THE CLOUD AND THE LINE ⸭ THE KINGDOM PRINCIPLES

PAUL CLAYTON GIBBS

BOOK TWO IN THE KINGDOM TRILOGY

Published by Harris House Publishing
Arlington, Texas
USA

Published in association with Pais Project Publications.

This title is also available in other formats.
Visit www.paisproject.bigcartel.com for ordering.

Requests for information should be addressed to: info@paisproject.com

Library of Congress Cataloging-in-Publication Data

Gibbs, Paul Clayton, 1964 -
      The Cloud and the Line: The Kingdom Principles / Paul Clayton Gibbs
         p.cm.
      Includes bibliographical references
      ISBN 978-0-9824160-2-0 (pbk.)
      1. Christianity and Culture. 2. Christian Life. I. Title.
BR115.C8G53   2011
261 - dc22   2011931914

the team
author paul clayton gibbs
project manager terry tamashiro harris
dictation & research brooke luby
editing & proofing terry tamashiro harris sebrina miller
design & typesetting paul green
publicity & promotion pais:global team
first draft feedback tom anthony karla & ron hagan terry roberts chris whitney kim driggers

for joel and levi
my favorite people
"remember the dream"

my thanks to

lynn || for proving that *"two are better than one for they have a better return for His work"*

terry || for all your wisdom, patience and hard work; it is such a privilege to work with you

brooke || for your belief in this book and for using your gift to make it happen

paul || for your continued dedication to the cause, your example and friendship

tifany || for your humble sacrifice of time, agenda and inspiring passion

mike || for making sure the teaching on these pages is applied to the schools of the world

burkharts || for pastoring my family during the writing of this book

kevin and ann || because you are reaping what you sowed into so many for so long

harris house publishing || for seeking God's Kingdom first and your business second

book project friends || for supporting this book and investing in its message

wayne, terry, kim, jim, claire, jules, matt, hannah, matthias, john, karen, beverly, norman, jimmy and jenny

pais directors i've worked with || for spreading these principles in the schools of the world

andy baimbridge, rachel eden, tina woodward, mike davies, steve and jenny webster, beccy and mark riley, adam islip, steve wilkinson, john kay, louise driess, rebecca bailey, sarah and nic mcbride, ben and gale dowding, pete and bryony baker, steve and vanessa keates, neil fearn, chris matthewman, emma ramsden, richard and sophie mcguiness, rob and keren johnson, kelli mcfarlane, steve and sebrina miller, ocke, andré springhut, tony puckett, stephanie medina, sally dorrington, robin frohnmayer, emma and chris cunnington, mark kernohan, jonny foster, mawunyo debrah, iain fogg and the foxy lynn

plus so many other directors that i have not had the pleasure of working with directly but who have kept the faith and shared in our journey to see His Kingdom come to the schools of the world

CONTENTS

PROLOGUE

favorites

God has no favorites.

Or so I'm told.

That's odd . . . because I would have never guessed it.

In fact, I would have thought just the opposite.

I would have almost been certain of the fact that He is partial to certain men or women because of the way He appears to treat them. It seems to me that sometimes two completely different people can do the same thing, and yet the repercussions can be vastly different.

I think of a hero like David the giant-slayer.

Here is someone whom we are told is:

> A man after God's own heart.[1]

Yet this same man committed adultery with a woman and then plotted the death of her husband. How is it then that he has such a special place in God's mind that even the Son of God is affectionately called the 'Son of David'?[2]

God must have favorites. What other explanation could there be?

But I am wrong. I must be. The Bible tells me so:

> There is no favoritism.[3]

> And masters, treat your slaves in the same way. Do not threaten them, since you know that he who is both their Master and yours is in heaven, and there is no favoritism with him.[4]

So if favoritism does not affect the way our King deals with us, then what does? Is He influenced at all by our 'Christian' label? Just how does God view morality, and what is His scale for ethical weights and measures?

christianized

It is a myth that Jesus hated all the religious people and loved all the sinners.

He invested in anyone who came to Him.

He chased no one.

Why? Because how you enter the presence of Jesus can decide who you are when you depart from it.

How we enter the Bible can often determine how we leave it.

Enter it looking for simple answers, and you will leave it with complex questions.

Enter it simply looking for life principles, and that is all you will leave it with.

Entering it that way will not give you the alternative life that Jesus spoke about. It will just give you the 'Christian version of' what everyone else is doing.

We will seek everything else the world seeks—wealth, happiness, security, respect—but we just do it the Christianized way.

And when it comes to advancing the Kingdom of God, the 'Christian version of' never works.

printer

When I was a teenager, I received a small red Bible. At the back was a list of possible life issues I might face—peer pressure, bullying, temptation, etc.

Each problem had a corresponding scripture. Each scripture was carefully selected to help answer my questions. I appreciate the sentiment, but I have a question.

Why do we feel compelled to present the Bible as having all the answers?

The Bible does not claim that it does.

Jesus never said it did. Neither did Paul or Matthew or any of the writers.

They said things like, "*all Scripture is God-breathed and is useful for teaching, rebuking, correcting and training in righteousness.*"[5]

But they also tell us that:

> *Jesus did many other things as well. If every one of them were written down, I suppose that even the whole world would not have room for the books that would be written.*[6]

So are we missing some important stuff?

As I got a little older, I was trained to tell others the Bible was the 'handbook to life.' That makes sense in a society that loves guidebooks and manuals. If God's intention, however, were to write a handbook to life, I am convinced He could have done a better job.

You see, when God has something to say, not only does He say it well, but whole planets are created and populated.

So was a self-help guide really His sole intention?

Should we really be just looking for simple rules and regulations?

I have heard it said that pagans sin by seeking fulfillment in *creation* rather than the *Creator*. Do Christians, however, make a parallel mistake?

Do we seek fulfillment in *answers* instead of the *Author*?

If so . . . why?

When I have finished writing this chapter, I will probably want to print it out. That won't be a problem because I have a printer. Operating my printer will not be a problem because I have a printer manual.

The great thing about my printer manual is I don't need to meet the inventor of the printer. I just need his book.

Perhaps if the Bible *did* have all the answers, then I would not need the Author.

Perhaps I'd like an operating manual.

Perhaps I could operate God.

book

To be really candid, I am concerned about this book.

I am concerned about how you *respond* to it.

My fear has little to do with whether you like the book or not, but rather with what you *think* I am trying to teach.

This is the second book in the Kingdom Trilogy, three books that teach about the kind of people who can change the world.

The first book, *The Line and the Dot,* presents alternative thoughts on *vision.* It shows the importance of going beyond the tried and trusted systems of the world to pioneer the new things that God puts in our hearts.

The third book, *The Seed and the Cloud,* will look at alternative thoughts on *direction*. It will teach us about the unusual processes that God uses to guide and shape us.

This second book, *The Cloud and the Line*, presents alternative thoughts on *religion*. It aims to help us understand the Spirit that resides in those who do not simply *believe* differently but *behave* differently.

To do so, it unpacks the principles and parables of Jesus in order to demonstrate what God favors from what He does not, what He rewards and what He does not, and what He punishes and what He does not.

And herein lies my problem.

My concern is that when hearing the Kingdom Principles, we may be tempted to see these six divine concepts as a package.

As leverage.

As a way of getting things from God.

We could then perhaps be seduced into thinking that this package contains six steps to twisting God's hand behind His back and forcing Him to "pay up." But this is not the intention of this book. I mention this because, as with the Bible, how you enter it can determine how you exit it.

Please understand—this is an *anti-self-help* book.

Still want to read on?

I hope you do. In doing so, you will discover six Kingdom Principles that teach us the dynamics of:

> *Seeking*
> *Judging*
> *Storing*
> *Using*
> *Reaping*
> *Humbling*

Each Kingdom Principle is split into three sections:

> *The Problem – because I have many when thinking through the vision God has given me.*

> *The Principle – because they outweigh, if not outnumber, the problems and help us all find a way forward.*

> *The Promise – because for those who seek the heart of the King, there are many new promises to be realized.*

The intent of this book is to empower you with a fresh way of thinking, and it is written in order that we may fulfill His dreams first and ours second.

THE HEART OF THE KING

battle

Knights fight for the heart of the King.

On my mother's side, I am a Munro, a Scottish clan whose allegiance to the king was legendary. As told in the story of the Battle of Bannockburn which occurred in the year 1314, Chief Robert Munro led the clan knights in support of King Robert the Bruce.

Robert the Bruce was an extremely well-loved king. When he died, he asked that his heart be cut out, embalmed, and given to a worthy knight who would take it to Jerusalem. His friend Douglas took up the challenge and wore it in a container around his neck. His men, knowing it was there, were inspired to fight with the same passion as Douglas.

One day, when backed into a corner by their enemy and feeling defeat was imminent, Douglas took an extraordinary action. He ripped the heart from around his neck and held it up so his men could see it. Then, with a huge cry, Douglas threw it deep behind the enemy's front line and shouted, *"Fight for the heart of the king!"*

Game on.

What a great story! I can just imagine these fanatical, fiercely loyal knights, bonded together over time by pledges and oaths, watching in desperation as the heart of their king was thrown so far away from them.

So far, yet so near.

I can only imagine what stirred within them. The passion! The anger! The rage! The spirit! What fighting must have ensued in their quest to rescue and retrieve that symbol of all they believed in and fought for!

The heart of Robert the Bruce is now entombed in Melrose Abbey, Scotland. Dead and buried, it will never be fought over again.

However, the heart of our King of kings is alive and well.

Will *it* ever be fought over again?

Will a new kind of knight rise up?

knights

Where have all the knights gone?

> *Put on the full armor of God so that you can take your stand against the devil's schemes. For our struggle is not against flesh and blood, but against the rulers, against the authorities, against the powers of this dark world and against the spiritual forces of evil in the heavenly realms.*[7]

I once read a magazine that said its greatest feedback had come from an article entitled, "Why Are Christian Men Such Wimps?"

That bothered me. I don't want to be a wimp. I don't want to flake out. I want to be a Gibbs.

Although I am English, my family name 'Gibbs' has Scottish origins. We are Picts, a warrior clan first mentioned in 297 AD as the 'painted or tattooed people.' In the film *King Arthur*, it is the Picts who decorated their bodies with vivid paint and tattoos and fought against the Roman invasion alongside Merlin.

We are the resistance. Our family crest consists of three battle-axes. (When I was a little boy, my father told me that these battle-axes represented my mother and two grandmothers.) The motto of the Gibbs' knights is 'firm of purpose.'

I do not want to be weak. I do not want to be a wimp. I want to be *firm of purpose.*

But what is my purpose? What is the purpose of a Christian? Is it to wage war on those with a different opinion? Is it to extend the boundaries of our faith through bloodshed and crusades? Is it to demand that others agree to the rules of our religion? Is it to follow a list of dos and don'ts?

Or, is our purpose found not on the battlefield but in the sky?

chivalry

Knights had a code of chivalry.

They lived above the line.

> *Chivalry: the concept of knighthood with its religious, moral, and social code; the combination of qualities expected of the ideal medieval knight, especially loyalty, courage, honor, courtesy, justice, and a readiness to help the weak.*[8]

They modeled the principles that all aspire to.

Knights rose above the average soldier, not just in fighting skills, but also in determination and loyalty. They pledged allegiance to a code of chivalry, banding together around a strong belief system. You could perhaps call them fanatics, but in truth, they simply committed themselves to live out the things that everyone else *said* they believed in.

The film *Kingdom of Heaven* is the brutal story of the fundamentally flawed Crusades and the knights who fought them. It is also an excellent visual image of the inward struggle between right and wrong.

Rights and wrongs.

There are two great scenes in the film, both involving oaths. In the first, the son visits his dying father. His father knights him, commanding an oath. He even slaps his son to ensure he remembers the command:

> *Be without fear in the face of your enemies.*
> *Be brave and upright that God may love thee.*
> *Speak the truth always, even if it leads to your death.*
> *Save for God the helpless and do no wrong.*
> *That is your oath.*
> > *[Father strikes his son across the face.]*
> *And that is so you will remember it.*[9]

In the second scene, the son is now leading the defense of the city of Jerusalem. A Hollywood bishop (a cowardly and weak-willed stereotype) points out that there are no knights. Vulnerable in the face of an onslaught, the son realizes the weight of the question: *Where have all the knights gone?*

The answer is that they all died fighting a fruitless, misguided battle. Now those that remained were huddled together in the city, desperately hoping for salvation.

In a great scene that is far more prophetic than the director probably realizes, the son turns to the bishop's young servant. He commands him to kneel and then recites the same oath spoken to him. Repeating his father's words, he slaps the servant's face and knights him.

The son then proceeds to get every willing, able-bodied man to kneel, and he knights the whole lot of them. The bishop sneeringly asks if knighting a man makes him a better fighter.

The music builds and the tension grows. The music stops and the answer follows:

"Yes."

I love it. What a great picture of the Kingdom!

The Father knights the Son, and then the Son knights all who bow the knee.

Jesus has also passed an oath onto us.

A philosophy for life.

A way to live.

A set of principles.

Jesus wants to knight *you.*

But there is one thing that you first need to realize. This one thing is the only obstacle in your way.

line-dwelling

There *is* a line.

Many Christians commit themselves to living on this line. I would describe this 'line-dwelling' as the way we *define* and *confine* ourselves by trying to work out what we can and cannot do as Christians—what we deem morally correct and morally wrong.

We create two extremes. At one end, we look for a cut-off point of what we can *get away with* before we reap the consequences. At the other end, we create a cut-off point of how far we *have to go* in order to gain the rewards we seek.

In our world of line-dwelling, we ask the simple questions.

On the subject of giving:

> *How much do I need to give to God in order to avoid chastisement?*
> *How much do I have to give to God to be considered generous?*

In the area of forgiveness:

> *What sins perpetrated against me do I have to forgive?*
> *How often should I forgive the perpetrator to be known as forgiving?*

In the area of entertainment:

> *What am I allowed to watch before I am judged as worldly?*
> *What rating can I get away with and still be called pure?*

It is as though we draw a line in the sand on certain subjects, and our faith then becomes a continual working out of our position. Once we have defined our position, we defend it as law against anybody who thinks differently.[10] Proving ourselves right becomes our mission, and so we go on exactly the wrong kind of crusade.

We are linear in our thinking and linear in our hearts.

But please notice: You cannot live above the line if there is no line to live above.

The Kingdom Principles are *not* anti-line.

They are a call to live above it.

hypnotize

Do you know how to hypnotize a chicken?

Simply force the chicken's head down so its beak touches the ground and its eyes are pointed at the floor. Then from the place where its beak touches the dirt, draw a line by walking backwards. The bird will be transfixed.

It will remain rooted to the spot, peering down the line you've created. It will not move. I guarantee it.[11]

Do you know how to hypnotize a human?

Do exactly the same thing.

Get them to look down and along the line. They too will become transfixed. They will struggle to move. You will both *define* and *confine* them.

We are called to soar like eagles, but we have been grounded like chickens.

cloud-dwelling

I love the Bible. I love it because with the right perspective, it draws me into the Author's presence.

In its words, the cloud represents the presence of God.

The *Shekhinah*.[12]

His Spirit. His heart. His mind.

> *He is represented in a pillar of cloud leading the Israelites.*
> *His presence is in a cloud that threw their enemies into confusion.*
> *He appeared in glory in a cloud.*
> *He speaks to Moses in a dense cloud.*

His presence appears as a cloud above the tabernacle.
He envelops the people as a cloud at Jesus' baptism.
He will arrive on a cloud in the second coming.
He will sit on a cloud at the time of judgment.[13]

This book is about cloud-dwelling. It encourages our hearts to be free from the heavy burdens that weigh us down. It will tell us that we can be birds of prey rather than birds of the farmyard.

This book addresses the thing that most breaks the King's heart . . . The heart-breaking servant who wimps out from the fight. A subject who is merely looking for easy answers and a simple moral code to live by.

This book hopes to convict us of foul language . . . Language that says, "Just tell me what to do, how far to go."

This book promises something more. And it is this *something more* that Jesus came to teach us. He trains us in these things through principles within parables. He teaches us to connect with the Father and one another through a new way. He makes us a new promise—that those who live in this new covenant can find the answer to a new kind of question:

What is really in the heart of my King?

How do I please Him? How do I fight for Him the way He wants me to fight? How can my moral compass lead me to do the right thing simply because it is the right thing? How do I avoid missing the point?

Because we *can* miss the point, can't we?

Please understand that like all clouds, this cloud casts a shadow . . . a line.

It is the religious or moral code, the rules and regulations.

Living in the shadow is better than living outside of it.

But please don't mistake it for living in Him.

KINGDOM PRINCIPLE 1 ✦ SEEK FIRST

1

I vow to make the Kingdom of God my primary concern,
knowing He will make it His to give me all I need.

KINGDOM PRINCIPLE 1

SEEK FIRST | | THE PROBLEM

swap

Stories.

They teach us so much.

One time a gang of thieves planned a jewelry heist. They were certain they could break into the shop, steal the jewelry, and vanish without a trace. They were even confident they could do it without setting off the alarm.

But there was a problem. They wouldn't be able to sell the stolen jewelry before the news of their crime had spread. So they came up with a solution.

In the middle of the night, they stealthily slipped into the store without tripping the security system. Carefully, they opened the glass cases that housed the most precious jewelry. Next, they opened the ones containing the least expensive items. And then . . .

They swapped the labels.

Over the next two days, members of the gang walked into the store in broad daylight to purchase rings, bracelets, and necklaces. These seemingly innocent customers bought costly items for mere pennies on the dollar, and they walked out making a small fortune.

I can just imagine the smirks on their faces as they not only celebrated their ingenious plot but also watched customers pay far too much for mere baubles.

And here is our problem.

Our spiritual enemy has done the same thing.

It's not simply those who do not know Jesus who have fallen for this trick. It is the Church. Jesus came to a people who were following God but investing in the wrong things and in the wrong way. They were blinded by their religion and the religion of those around them.

We need to swap back the labels.

paganism

History.

It teaches us so little.

It should teach us so much, but it does not.

If we miss its context, we miss its point.

> *So do not worry, saying, 'What shall we eat?' or 'What shall we drink?' or 'What shall we wear?' For the pagans run after all these things, and your heavenly Father knows that you need them.*[14]

Jesus said, *"For the pagans run after these things,"* inferring that we should not.

Did He simply mean we shouldn't seek fulfillment in worldly possessions? Or was He getting at something deeper, more specific?

Without *His* context, we miss *His* point.

Consider the word 'pagan.' I used to think it was someone who worshipped Satan and ate babies for breakfast. Generally, however, I presumed pagans were those who totally ignored God and ran after worldly possessions.

I couldn't have been more wrong. With the proper context, paganism takes on a whole new meaning. Let me explain.

The Talking Heads were correct. There is a 'road to nowhere.' It is in Turkey. And it's called the 'Sacred Way.'[15] This ancient roadway is fifteen miles long and goes nowhere. Archeologists teach us that roadside shops, monumental tombs, baths, fountains, and rest stops once lined its entire route. Even today, statues of important people adorn the path.[16]

This road had significance.

And yet the Sacred Way does not lead to a city or a town or even a village. It did not transport people to an important trade center or strategic port. There was no campus of education, no Olympic-sized sporting venue, nor athlete's village.

So why was such a well-used road built to allow people to travel a long day's walk from the nearest town? It led to Apollo's temple at Didyma. And something *very* peculiar took place there.

For the pagans, what happened at the end of the Sacred Way was a very big deal. And Jesus knew it.

You came here for the 'Oracle of God.'

oracle

An oracle is a message from a god that answered a specific question. The word itself also refers to the medium who gives the message as well as the shrine where the answer is given.[17]

As the pagans approached the temple, their hearts beat faster. They were approaching Apollo, the god of music and light.

After washing themselves in the well, they would hand an animal to a priest who would ceremonially sacrifice it on the outside altar. They hoped their offering would earn them the opportunity to ask the oracle a question. Digging through its entrails, Apollo's servants would give them a *yes* or a *no*. If the answer was 'yes,' then with apprehension and trembling, through a mixture of fear and excitement, they would approach the temple steps and wait for the gigantic door to open. Dramatically and to the sound of a drum, another priest would open the doors from within. He would be dressed as Apollo: robed in white and adorned in pure gold. A truly awesome sight.

The pilgrims would bow down and ask their questions. Then the door would close and they would wait for an answer.

Sometimes for *days*.

Sometimes for *weeks*.

Sometimes for *months*.

Sometimes for *years*.[18]

Inside the temple was a smaller temple known as a *naiskos*. Inside the naiskos was a sight you had to see to believe.

There, suspended over an open pit, sitting in a tripod, was Apollo's oracle. Usually an older woman, she was surrounded by disciples and was in some type of chemically-induced trance. While in this hypnotic state, the oracle would give her answer, Apollo's answer, to a priest who would write it down in a form of poetry. A message would then go out to the waiting pilgrims that the oracle was about to be given.[19]

Eagerly—perhaps frantically—they would rush to the temple doors. They were about to hear a word from *god!*

But what kind of question did these pagans ask?

And how is the way they pursued their god different from the way Jesus wants us to seek Him?

questions

Their inquiry might be a question of romance or money.

It might be that they were considering a career change:

> *Would Apollo tell me if this would please him or not?*

Or maybe, as in one famous case, the request would concern a military campaign:

> *If a king goes to war, will he win or lose?*

The answers could be ambiguous. In the case of Croesus, King of Lydia, he asked Apollo's oracle whether or not he would defeat Persia if he fought them. Eventually the oracle replied, *"A nation will fall."*

Great. Thanks for the advice. And can I have my sheep back please?

All that time spent waiting for one ambiguous word from a god, and yet we have an entire book full of wisdom!

Our book, the Bible, is not ambiguous. But for its answers to be truly understood, it does require the *right kind of questions.* Jesus was telling us that our questions should be different from the pagans' questions. And here is where Jesus' point might be missed.

What separates a follower of Christ and a pagan is not that one seeks divine advice and one does not. The difference between the two is the *kind* of question they ask.

> Pagan: *"Lord, if I do this, will you bless me?"*
> Follower of Jesus: *"Lord, what are you doing, and how can I bless you?"*

Paganism is not simply a rejection of God to seek worldly things. It is seeking worldly things *via* God.

Sound familiar?

The devil has swapped the labels.

We value the wrong kind of question too highly and the right kind of question too lightly. And the things we value too lightly are the things for which we are not prepared to sacrifice.

This poses the following question.

When Jesus returns, how will He see those whose primary reason for following Him is a better lifestyle?

Will He see them as disciples . . . or pagans?

eternity

Jesus had a problem.

He was recruiting children to change the world, but God's children were following their God in the same way that the world was following theirs. He had to change the way their minds ticked and their hearts beat. And so, through words,

He began to paint the most wonderful picture ever painted—a true picture of the Kingdom of Heaven.

This leads me to the problem It is another problem of context. This one even has a cliché

> *There is a God-shaped hole inside all of us that only God can fill.*

But what if that is only a half-truth? What if there is more to that thought?

It seems truer to say that *in this life:*

> *There is a God-shaped hole inside all of us that even God cannot fill!*

The Pais Project is the organization I founded in 1992. One division of it places missionaries in schools all around the world. We train young people how to pursue God and then equip them to make missionaries of students.[20] I am concerned that, as I make missionaries who make missionaries, all I may pass on is a selfish faith—a religion summed up by the teaching that we must not fill the gap with wealth, possessions, sex, drugs, or rock and roll, but pursue God for happiness instead.

I am just not sure that was the message of Jesus either.

Why?

> *He has also set eternity in the hearts of men.*[21]

What an amazing thought! God has placed eternity in our hearts.

We are eternal creatures . . . He put eternity in our hearts before He sent death into our world. We have hopes, desires, needs, and a destiny that go beyond this life.

We are eternal creatures . . . Therefore, there will always be something missing in this temporal life. God can only fulfill our deepest longings in the eternity that eternity will provide.

The purpose of our lives is not to fulfill *our* desires in the *correct* way, but to fulfill *His* desires in *His* way.

We should be knights pursuing His cause, but our message has simply become that the key to happiness is choosing the right god.

I can understand why this has happened. Everyone on the planet is searching for something, because eternity was placed within us all. Yet instead of seeking God and His Kingdom, we search elsewhere.

Perhaps a sacrificial offering to anything other than God is easier. Oracles don't follow us up on our promises or poke around in our lives asking us awkward questions.

We need to swap the labels back and re-teach Jesus' message of the Kingdom *first*.

If this is not taught and embraced by a new generation, then my problem will be realized:

Another crusade of missionaries passing on a religion of self and self-help.

Another confused and misused cohort of naturally passionate young people will rise up, desperate to cram into their lives every spiritual tool they can use to fill something that can never be filled.

second

A people who seek first *second* will never fully experience God's provision supplied His way. What happens then?

How can a person who has never fully experienced God's consistent provision have the renewable faith to carry on consistently?

How can a person who has never consistently experienced God's Kingdom dynamics pass on faith to others?

And if they cannot pass on real faith, then what kind of faith will they pass on?

> *For you cross land and sea to make one convert, and then you turn that person into twice the child of hell you yourselves are!* [22]

Yes, there is a war. Yes, there is a battle. Yes, we do need knights. But no, we don't need another misguided crusade with a flawed understanding of how to create the Kingdom of God on earth.

Most Christian teaching suggests that what is in our *heads* must drop several inches into our *hearts*.

The teaching of this book says that there is something in our *hearts* that needs to rise several inches into our *heads*.

questions to ask

Am I simply Christianizing my life?

Am I simply seeking the Christian version of what the world is seeking?

Why will this not advance God's purpose in my life?

What labels have been swapped in my life?

Which of these two questions do I ask most:

> *"Lord, if I do this, will you bless me?"*

> *"Lord, what are you doing, and how can I bless you?"*

What is my primary reason for following Jesus?

Do I have desires that might only be fulfilled in eternity?

If so, what are they?

How can I decide if I have fully experienced God's consistent provision?

How can I have the renewable faith to carry on consistently?

What kind of faith am I passing on to those I love?

How does eternity affect my daily choices?

questions to add:

KINGDOM PRINCIPLE 1

SEEK FIRST || THE PRINCIPLE

wish

Knights go on a quest.

> During harvest time, three of the thirty chief men came down to David
> at the cave of Adullam, while a band of Philistines was encamped in the
> Valley of Rephaim. At that time David was in the stronghold, and the
> Philistine garrison was at Bethlehem. David longed for water and said,
> "Oh, that someone would get me a drink of water from the well near the
> gate of Bethlehem!" So the three mighty men broke through the Philistine
> lines, drew water from the well near the gate of Bethlehem and carried it
> back to David. But he refused to drink it; instead, he poured it out before
> the LORD. "Far be it from me, O LORD, to do this!" he said. "Is it not the
> blood of men who went at the risk of their lives?" And David would not
> drink it.
>
> Such were the exploits of the three mighty men.[23]

I love to picture this story of King David sitting around the fire with his best
friends after a long day at battle. He seems to sigh, as I might after a hard
day's work in Dallas when I say, *"I could kill for a Chicken Tikka Masala from
Manchester's Curry Mile,"* or *"What I'd give for pudding and chips from the local
chippy in Moston."*

It's wishful thinking.

Imagine a small fire casting shadows on the faces of those huddled around it. As
David yearns, "Oh, for a drink from Bethlehem's well," I picture his three most lov-
ing supporters give knowing glances to one another. Silently, they reach for their
swords and stealthily slip into the darkness. After a seemingly suicidal mission
battling through enemy lines to the source of David's desire, and after an equally
courageous return trip, they give David what seems to be the shock of his life.

They present to him what he longed for.

The king's response reveals a heart touched by their action. So shocked is he that,
as was a common custom, he pours out the water as a drink offering to God.

His friends had gone *above* and *beyond.*

Or, as one author wrote:

The king's *wish* had become their *command.*[24]

quest

Has God's wish become your command?

Or are you looking for written instructions signed, sealed, and delivered in triplicate?

He wishes for us to be moved by what moves Him, rather than by being told what to do.

But to know what moves Him, we must look into His heart. In His heart are principles, and one principle is foundational.

It glues all the others together and is found in the book of Matthew.[25]

> *But seek first his kingdom and his righteousness, and all these things will be given to you as well.* (NIV)

> *But seek ye first the kingdom of God, and his righteousness; and all these things shall be added unto you.* (KJV)

> *And He will give you all you need from day to day if you live for Him and make the Kingdom of God your primary concern.* (NLT)

If there is a secret to life, it is this:

We must make the Kingdom of God our primary concern and trust that God will take care of the rest.

The Kingdom of God was central to the teaching of Jesus. Over one hundred references to the Kingdom occur in the four gospels, and many of them are found in Jesus' parables. To understand this secret, however, we must first understand what the Kingdom of God actually is.

The New Testament Greek word used for the Kingdom of God/Heaven is *Basileia*.[26] It means 'royalty, reign, rule, and realm.'

Therefore, the Kingdom of God is a life, community, nation, or world where God's royalty is undisputed, where hearts are fully given to His reign, where He rules unchallenged, and where His realm is clearly seen by all. The Kingdom of God on earth is His dream for us, for the world.

So what is Jesus asking of us?

It is this: to make *His* dream *our* dream.

amidah

Seeking first means that God's dream must consume us holistically.

One day, a disciple of Jesus asked his Rabbi what appears to be an odd request.

> *Lord, teach us how to pray.*[27]

This begs the question: Did they honestly not know?

Of course they did.

The disciples grew up in Galilee in a deeply religious and prayerful community. They had far more prayers and times of intercession than many of us.

Again, context helps. Their request was the kind all disciples would ask of their particular rabbi. The Jews had, and still have today, certain daily prayers. Perhaps the most significant is the Amidah, a long and articulate set of eighteen benedictions that takes five minutes for a fluent Hebrew speaker to recite quickly.

A common practice was for a rabbi to teach their talmidim, or disciples, their own personal condensed version. Americans would call it the *Cliff Notes of the Amidah*.

These edited prayers only contained elements, sound bites, and highlights. They were designed to help communicate their rabbi's understanding of God's priorities.

So in reality, the question Jesus was being asked was this:

> *Can you teach us what God considers most important in our daily prayers?*

When Jesus complies, notice His priority is listed as the *first* request:

> *Your kingdom come, your will be done, on earth as it is in heaven.*[28]

What is Jesus actually asking us to pray here? A careful examination tells us that *'your Kingdom come'* is an exhortation which means 'Rule, God, over more and more individuals.' His dream was to be their first thought, the prayer on their lips, and their only way ahead.

Jesus is emphasizing the fact that the kinds of people who will make up the Kingdom of God are those who want His Kingdom to come more than anything else in life!

Is that me?

Is that you?

Are you the kind of person who in Jesus' eyes will make up the Kingdom of Heaven?

line

Jesus said, *"For where your treasure is, there your heart will be also."*[29]

On-the-line thinking wastes time on whether or not to tithe.[30] It spends too much energy wondering if it should tithe on its net income or its gross income. The ancient principle instead asks, *How and where do I give most to advance the Kingdom of God?*

Whether or not the command to tithe is still valid, we miss the point when we argue. God is not looking for *more* or *less*, He is looking for *generosity*.

Giving is a particular discipline that stores up treasure in heaven, not simply for us to look forward to receiving, but as a war chest from which God funds His campaign to destroy the works of the devil.

If you are passionate about His campaign, you will put it *first* in your budget.

When it comes to their treasure, line-dwellers are motivated by *their* questions:

> *Do I have to give?*
> *How much is required?*
> *What guarantees will I get in return?*

Cloud-dwellers, however, are moved by *His* questions:

> *How much do you love Me?*
> *How often do you dream My dream?*
> *What price tag would you put on it?*

Cloud-dwellers give with an understanding that what they give is not a tax to keep them safe.

They are not paying the spiritual mafia.

This is not protection money.

mite

The Kingdom of God is upside down, inside out, and back to front.

In our world, we measure the worth of something by how much we give for it. In the Kingdom of Heaven, value is measured differently. God measures the worth of something by how much we hold back.

We place significance on how much money was *exchanged*; heaven places significance on how much was *retained*.

When Jesus points out a model of Kingdom giving, He compares a widow who gives very little compared to a wealthy man who gives a lot. He favors the widow not for what she gave, but for what she had leftover . . . *nothing.*

> *"All these people gave their gifts out of their wealth; but she out of her poverty put in all she had to live on."* [31]

King David also demonstrated a Kingdom heart because he understood this.

One day he approached a landowner and asked him for a plot of land on which to build an altar to God. The man was blown away that the king would request something of his, and so he offered the land for no payment.

David did not accept.

His reply tells us why.

> *"I will not take for the LORD what is yours, or sacrifice a burnt offering that costs me nothing."* [32]

How do we measure if the Kingdom of God is our primary concern?

Not by what we give, but by what we have leftover.

aspiration

One of the problems for those of us who claim to be seeking first the Kingdom of God is that we are often taught to seek first *second*. Instead of our primary vision being the Kingdom of God, we are advised to spend much of our time looking at things to avoid.

As I wrote, in my previous book, *The Line and the Dot*, avoiding sin is like driving a Formula 1 race car. If we spend too much time concentrating on the curb, we will either hit it or move so far away from it that we hit the opposite curb of legalism.

Seeking first enables us instead to focus on the invisible perfect driving line.

In 2010, Bill Gates' wife, Melinda, spoke on how non-profit organizations could learn a thing or two from companies like Coca-Cola®. In her TEDx conference speech, she advised the idealists of the world to stop preaching *avoidance* and instead preach *aspiration*. [33]

Avoidance, she said, sounds like this: "Use a condom; don't get AIDS. Wash your hands; don't get diarrhea."

Melinda hit upon an ancient Biblical truth.

> *Where there is no vision, the people cast off restraint.*[34]

She shared how, in the past, in order to prevent open defecation on the streets of Northern India, toilets were provided along with signs warning people to use them to avoid disease. The attempt was unsuccessful.

More recently, they utilized aspiration by marketing the toilet as a trendy tool in winning a wife. The campaign was not only ingenious, but successful. Newspapers reported their victory using headlines such as, *"No loo, no I do"* and, *"Show us your loo before you woo."*

In another part of the world, Melinda Gates showed pictures of her husband sitting with smiling young men who were waiting to be circumcised.

Telling men to have an operation in order to avoid HIV failed; the aspiration of a better sex life succeeded. Apparently, the men have been taught that women prefer a man who has been circumcised.

To some, these methods may seem in poor taste, but they worked. Lives were saved.

Follow this Kingdom Principle and you will no longer be hypnotized by avoidance. You will no longer stare at a line which asks, "What should I avoid in order to avoid a bad thing happening?"

Instead, you will aspire to dream the dream that Jesus dreams.

You will become fearless!

You will receive the gift of faith.

Not a flaky faith with lots of zest, but little passion. Not a scaredy-cat spirituality with many convictions, but little hope. Not a double-minded life easily blown from one thing to another, with many dreams, but little vision.

No. Instead, you will fight the good fight and inspire others to do the same.

merimnao

To prepare us for the challenge of the *Seek First* Kingdom Principle, Jesus pre-empts our fears with some advice.

> *". . . Do not worry . . . "*[35]

At first this sounds simplistic, but actually He is passing on very specific wisdom.

He uses a word translated into the Greek as *merimnao* meaning 'to divide into pieces, to be distracted.'[36]

Jesus was preparing us, quite literally saying, "Do not go to pieces!"

It is good advice. Juggling many desires will cause you to live a fractured life.

He wants us to see the bigger picture.

A good illustration is the well-known story of the professor who stands in front of his class with a large transparent jar.[37] He fills his jar to the brim with rocks and asks his eager students whether the jar is full. They reply:

Yes.

With a gentle smile, he then pours pebbles into the jar. They run into the cracks in between the rocks and fill it to the top. "Is it full now?" he asks his intrigued onlookers.

Ah. Yes.

To the students' bemusement, he then pours sand into the container. "What about now?"

Erm. We think so.

The fourth time, the professor pours water into the jar.

"Now it is fully filled," he tells them. "So what do you think the point of this object lesson is?"

One student, missing the point, replied, "No matter how busy you are, you can always fit in something else."

Correcting him, his teacher made his message clear saying:

"Unless you put the big rocks in first, you'll never fit them in at all."

Jesus' dream is a very big rock. It is unmovable. It is going to happen. His proposal to us is quite simply:

Do we want to be involved?

Now you must think seriously about that question, because this rock is too big to fit into your life *after* your dreams of wealth, your worries of persecution, your plans for pleasure, and your fears of trouble.

Jesus said those dreams and fears might even choke His dream right out of you.[38]

If the Kingdom of God is not the first thing in the jar, it is impossible to squeeze it in after everything else.

In fact, it would be easier for a camel to squeeze through the eye of a needle.

trap

Cloud-dwelling is intangible.

Line-dwelling is not.

The fact that line-dwelling is so tangible is exactly what makes it so attractive. Living on the line means you don't have to wrestle with a God who can feel slippery at times. In fact, line-dwelling is so tangible that it also encourages us to hold onto things we should not.

Alternatively, it is hard to live according to the Kingdom Principles because it requires an act of faith that goes well beyond trusting in the things we can see, hear, touch, and taste.

In my early days of ministry, to present the dynamics of faith to school children with no religious background, I resorted to many visual aids. One of my favorites involved a large rat trap with ferocious metal teeth. I would ask, "Who is brave enough to trust me?" Then I would have a courageous volunteer place a long piece of paper into the trap.

CRASH! The metal teeth slammed shut as the startled student screamed and laughed. Thinking he had proven himself, the student would walk back toward his seat, but I would beckon him to return. I would then ask the class, "Do you think he really trusts me?"

"No!" they would shout.

"Then what else could he do to prove he trusts me?"

Without fail, someone would say, "Put his finger in it!" as the class roared with approval. I would first act shocked and then encourage the student to put his finger in my rat trap, challenging him to trust me to keep him safe. After a great deal of dramatic build up, the student, or a substitute volunteer if the student had backed out, would tentatively put his finger in.

You could hear a pin drop and would have heard the metal teeth crash, but of course, they never did.

The class would applaud the pale-faced volunteer, who always had a little more color in his cheeks than the supervising school teacher. Then I would show them the tiny catch on the rat trap that was in place the first time, but which I secretly disabled with sleight of hand for the 'finger version.'

Seeking first involves trusting a principle that Jesus trusted in, even when every physical circumstance shouts, "No!"

The only person in the room who knew all the facts was me. I was able to ask the students to do the unthinkable because I was in full possession of all the details.

For that moment,

In that class,

Regarding that event,

I was omniscient.

To seek first the Kingdom of God, we need to understand that God knows everything. He is in possession of all the facts.

> *Spiritual maturity:* the quiet confidence that God is in control.[39]

The quest Jesus invites us on is exciting. It is a journey of faith. It does not take shortcuts, but the journey itself is fun. And it goes on for eternity.

The rat race, however, offers only momentary rewards.

It has its very own rat trap—the trap that says great blessing will come to those who have to see to believe. Or, to put it another way, to those who seek to do deals with God.

> *"Because you have seen me, you have believed; blessed are those who have not seen and yet have believed."*[40]

Seeing is believing, but believing without seeing is blessed.

The cloud . . .

Or the line . . .

Where do you dwell?

things to learn

My King has a quest for me to go on.

He wants His wish to be my command.

He does not want me to look for written instructions delivered in triplicate.

The New Testament Greek word for the Kingdom of God/Heaven is *Basileia*.

It means *rule, reign, royalty*, and *realm*.

Jesus spoke about the Kingdom over 100 times; it was His favorite subject.

The Lord's Prayer is Jesus' summary of the most important Jewish prayer.

Seeking first the Kingdom of God is the foundational principle.

Those who will make up the Kingdom are those who want His Kingdom to come.

And they want it more than anything else.

I must make the Kingdom of God my primary concern.

To do this, I make His Kingdom the big rock of my life that all else fits around.

And then I trust that God will take care of the rest.

Unless I put the big rock of the Kingdom in first, I will never fit it in at all.

He judges whether I am doing this not by what I give but by what I have left over.

additional notes:

KINGDOM PRINCIPLE 1

SEEK FIRST || THE PROMISE

exercise

Question: Can you envision a life like this?

A life where the role of a husband is not so much to put food on the table but to make sure his family is in the will of God, trusting that if it is, God will ensure there is bread on the table.

A life where, as a single person, your decisions are not dictated by your search for a partner but your pursuit of God, convinced that along the way, He will find you the right spouse.

A life where, as a leader, your responsibility is not to grow your organization but to put God's priorities as number one in its agenda and budget, trusting that He will grow what you lead.

How freeing would that feel?

Jesus is inviting you and me on a quest to make things on earth how things are in heaven.

> *Christianity is not simply living for Jesus; it is living for the things that Jesus lived for.*

> *Christianity is not simply believing in Jesus; it is believing in the things that Jesus believed in.*

> *Christianity is not simply having faith in Jesus; it is having faith in the things that Jesus had faith in.*

> *Christianity is not simply trusting in Jesus; it is trusting in the principles Jesus has entrusted to us.*

His Kingdom Principles.

My favorite English version of this foundational principle of *Seek First* is the New Living Translation. I think it illustrates what Jesus had in mind more clearly than the others.

And He will give you all you need from day to day if you live for Him and make the Kingdom of God your primary concern.

Try this exercise.

First, picture your local community or school or supermarket or factory or office. Then, imagine that everything going on in that place is happening as things happen in heaven.

What visual images come to mind when you think of Jesus' command to love God and love one another displayed at your local Wal-Mart?

What footage do you see when you visualize His grace and mercy dominating your local neighborhood?

What scenarios play out in your imagination if His level of honesty, integrity, and ethics were tantamount in your work place?

What do you see?

If you make that vision your top priority in life, then you are *seeking first*.

And if you do this, His promise is for you. If you do not, it is not.

He is looking for opportunities to reward us. His gifts are bespoke, made to measure, perfect.

Precise, yet generic.

Specific, yet holistic.

We cannot create these opportunities by seeking the blessings but by seeking His dream. And when we do seek His dream first, He always seems to add a cheeky little extra something.

Just as the *Seek First* principle applies to every area of our lives, so too does the promise that comes with it. Remember, however, that sometimes His promises don't turn out as we expect.

stuff

Application #1: *Seek first, and He will reward you with what money cannot buy.*

In the years I have spent following God, sometimes making His Kingdom my primary concern, and at other times not, I may have discovered a little of how the dynamic works.

I think it goes something like this:

> *God may not give you the money people use to buy stuff, but He will give you the stuff people use money to buy.*
>
> *He may not make you rich, but He will give you the security wealthy people hope to own.*
>
> *He may not give you a fast car, but He will give you the respect people purchase fast cars to gain.*
>
> *He may not give you the fame, but He will give you the influence that politicians can only dream about.*[41]

That's how His promise works. In the last twenty or so years, I have seen this play out in so many ways, and the stuff He provides is made to an individual's specifications.

For instance, He knows the thing that flicks my switch is adventure. I love skiing, surfing, sailing, and travelling. Below I've listed some of the adventures God has provided for me outside of the blessing of a wonderful family.

> I qualified as a sports scuba diver and explored various parts of Europe.
> I skied and snowboarded in both the Canadian and American Rockies.
> I sailed the Greek Islands on a schooner from Athens to Mount Olympus.
> I played in a rock band around the UK and recorded songs I've written.
> I surfed in some of the greatest surf spots in the world.
> I lived for several weeks in Barbados near its most exclusive beach.
> I have kayaked in Deep Cove and on the Yampa River.
> I have ridden an elephant in Thailand.

This sampling of my adventures may seem unimpressive if you come from a wealthy area or don't have a passion for these things. For me, however, I fulfilled my rather deep bucket list a long time ago and am now drawing up a new one.

What makes this list more impressive is the fact that my ministry has meant living off a small income, at times even falling below the poverty line. Many items on the list came as gifts, but most happened as part of my adventure. You could almost say they happened *because* I was doing the things to advance the Kingdom of God.

Many people will have done the things I have done. Yet how many will look back and know that to achieve them, they made the Kingdom second, third, or fourth on their priority list?

Better to do the fun stuff because you seek first than to do it because you don't.

Just a thought.

damsels

Application #2: *Seek first, and He will fight the battle for you.*

Every knight needs a damsel for whom to fight.

I believe partnership makes people, and whom you spend time with is, to some degree, who you eventually become. As far as I am concerned, choosing whom you marry is the second most important decision you will ever make in your life.

An on-the-line question asks: *Is he or she a Christian?*

A cloud-dwelling question asks: *Will this person join me in seeking first the Kingdom of God?*

There is a difference. One ticks a box. The other fulfills the spirit of the box.

After years of various relationships, at age twenty-one, I pledged to seek God before any woman. And to only seek a woman who sought God before she sought me.

A year or so later, I met Lynn.

In the first book of the Kingdom trilogy, *The Line and the Dot*, I tell a little of our story, including our first date when we backed into a police car and the weird incidents that confirmed she was *the one*. Essentially, I concluded she loved God and was really serious about following Him. The book skipped what happened next and concentrated on my vision, but I would like to stop here to give you the full story.

I had at one time felt I would be a missionary (only realizing later that it was a call to *make* missionaries). I wanted to train and then go somewhere in the world, maybe to Papua New Guinea or Asia.

Lynn split up with me, knowing she was not called to the same vision to which I thought I was. So I made the choice to pursue the step God had put in front of me—a missionary training course in Scotland. I was placed with the other trainees in an old stately home in the middle of nowhere. In fact, the nearest fish and chip shop was fifteen minutes away. Those circumstances may not seem bad to you, but what made things difficult was a real sense of loneliness. I was missing my one true love who was pretty upset with me.

Our phone conversations did not help. They went something like this:

> Me: *How are you?*
> Lynn: *Fine.*
> Me: *Oh, em, what have you been doing today?*
> Lynn: *Nothing.*
> Me: *I see . . . and how's your family?*
> Lynn: *Ok.*

I hope you can feel the awkwardness.

Eventually, I realized I was doing myself no good. I decided to pray and fast, and if I should forget Lynn, I would.

I opened my Bible at my scheduled reading for the day:

Two are better than one, because they have a good return for their work: If one falls down, his friend can help him up. But pity the man who falls and has no one to help him up! Also, if two lie down together, they will keep warm. But how can one keep warm alone? Though one may be overpowered, two can defend themselves. A cord of three strands is not quickly broken.[42]

I was confused. It seemed as though instead of helping me forget my 'ex,' I was being encouraged that she might be God's choice for me after all. In my naivety, I quickly phoned Lynn to tell her the 'good news.' She was, to state the obvious, not impressed.

She went very quiet when I read the passage out to her and then put the phone down on me.

After a long story, which is told in the next book of the trilogy, I returned home and immediately went to see Lynn.

She would not talk to me.

Twelve days later, we were engaged to be married.

It turns out that God was taking care of things. On the same day I read the passage in Ecclesiastes . . . so did Lynn!

Imagine her surprise after she read in her morning devotions, *"two are better than one, because they have a good return for their work,"* to then get a call out of the blue from me, effectively using it as a marriage proposal. The 'coincidence' alone did not convince her. But it helped.

In the twelve days after my arrival home, some peculiar things happened.

I had become convinced that we were to marry, but Lynn was still struggling with the enormity of the decision and perhaps what kind of life it might mean. The King, however, was still fighting my battle for me. On the eleventh day, we were walking through Manchester city centre, along Deansgate, amongst the heavy traffic, busy shops, and high-rise offices. Just as we passed the library holding the oldest fragment of the Bible in the world, Lynn turned to me and said:

"If we turn this corner and see a wedding, I will marry you."

I realized by her statement that she would go to great lengths to assure me that I had it wrong. As we exited the corner however, God showed me to what extent He would go to convince us He was right.

There in front of us, in the middle of a crossroad, was the whitest wedding you have ever seen.

Stunned is not the word.

I lived in Manchester for forty years and walked the city centre streets perhaps a thousand times in my adult life. I had never seen a wedding in Manchester city centre before. And I never saw one after.

That day, we bought the ring.

So what is His promise? Seek first the Kingdom of God, and He will give you all that you need.

Notice this intriguing verse from the passage that Lynn and I read on the same day:

A cord of three strands is not quickly broken.

The third strand that binds a marriage together can be many things—fear of loneliness, insecurity, low self-esteem, children, sex, and so on.

Make God your third strand instead, and you will be empowered.

Fight as His knight, and He will fight for you.

Oh, and by the way, after we were married, I found out that her family name on her mother's side is . . .

Lancelot.

mansion

Application #3: *Seek first, and He will hide things not* from *you but* for *you.*

My damsel and I have plenty of stories.

One of them is again partially referred to in *The Line and the Dot*. However, that covers only the first half of a series of extraordinary events concerning 234 Kenyon Lane, Moston, Manchester. In the first book, I told how sticking to our principle of free apprenticeships had dramatically restricted our income. I wrote of the bizarre tale that started with a murder and ended with the local government giving us just under $100,000 in order to rebuild the dilapidated house that we owned. The renovation added more rooms, a new garden, modern amenities, and more value to the 100 year old home.

Sometimes, God's promises consist of things He provides, and yet they also can consist of things He takes away.

After six years of living in our brand new home in a small community of four rebuilt streets, a predictable problem arose. The city council had poured millions into bricks and mortar, but the area labelled "a ghetto of underprivileged underachievers" was just as bad as always.[43] The millions they spent could not deal with the real problems. Financial answers don't work when the questions being asked are spiritual ones.

After spending millions on our area, the local authorities decided to knock it all down and land bank it. Essentially, the government bought us out. As good as this was, what they offered was still far less than what was needed to buy a similar house in a reasonable neighborhood.

Had we come to the end of God's promises?

As I said, sometimes God provides by shutting down options. For instance, we were offered an additional grant to help purchase another house, but the house we chose happened to be just outside the area that the grant covered.

After looking at many other houses, we finally found a suitable one within the parameters, and no one had bid on it for six months. When we offered to pay a little under the advertised price, a new buyer came along and began a bidding war we could not win. The owner of the house sent a message of apology, informing us that our competitor had offered to pay "whatever it took."

Not long after this door shut, a new and very surprising one opened—an invitation to move to America.

Through a set of peculiar circumstances that included a record high currency exchange that made the pound almost double the dollar, the low cost of housing in Texas, and some unexpected financial help, we were able to purchase a home beyond our wildest dreams.

We went from a small terraced house to a large four bedroom 'mansion.'

A short time after wondering if we would ever be able to buy a home equivalent to the one we had to leave, we moved into a house with a walk-in wardrobe almost the same size as our previous bedroom. It had a garden in the front and the back, and a study for me bigger than any of the rooms in our old house. And to cap it all, to add insult to my enemy's injury . . .

It had a swimming pool.

Seek first the Kingdom, and He may hide the good stuff from you in order to give you the best.

Even as I write this, I still struggle to get my mind around how it all worked out. To finish this story, let me tell you the weird bit. On my first visit back to the UK, I drove past the last house, the one the bidder had offered "whatever it took." There was no one living in it and no 'for sale' or 'for let' sign. Instead, a rather peculiar notice simply read: "For inquiries ring this number."

And so, being the inquisitive type, I inquired.

The house had been bought by a builder who, with a profuse use of profanities, told me:

"I don't know what to do with that house. I drove past it about a year ago and something told me I had to stop my car and buy it. So I slipped a note through the door, offering the owner anything he asked for it. It is so confusing; I am not sure what to do with it."

It is true to say God does not hide things *from* us, but *for* us.

The life of seeking first the Kingdom of God has many blind spots, but it is ultimately the greatest view from which to see the world!

trumps

Application #4: *Seek first, and receive wisdom you can use for a lifetime.*

An example of great cloud thinking in the Bible came from Daniel.[44]

Here is a young man torn away from his home to serve a foreign king. The Jews were carried away into captivity, but this handsome knight carried the Kingdom in his heart and its principles in his head.

Many of Daniel's qualities are well known. He was qualified, competent, and physically perfect. But almost hidden in this list of attributes is the description, 'quick to understand.'[45]

When Daniel is given food sacrificed to idols that he knows will displease his God, he refuses to eat it but suggests an alternative:

"Please test your servants for ten days: Give us nothing but vegetables to eat and water to drink. Then compare our appearance with that of the young men who eat the royal food, and treat your servants in accordance with what you see."[46]

An agreement is made. He is tested and found to be healthier than anyone else. From that moment on, he grows in wisdom and stature.

Now, how did he know what to do? How did he guess what would happen?

He had been given no prophecy or specific guideline in the law about how to deal with this kind of incident. He did not need one. He understood a principle.

In doing so, he gains wisdom that is *transferable*.

Prophecies don't shape us. Principles do.

Prophecies are just another form of circumstance. They are very useful for the moment or the situation to which they apply, but they are not good for much else.

A Kingdom Principle trumps a prophecy in that it teaches you *how* to think, not *what* to think.

A Kingdom Principle trumps a law in that it is transferable.

Cloud-dwellers recognize a Kingdom Principle. Daniel was a cloud-dweller, and this was not the only time he used this code in his conduct.

Remember the story of the lion's den?

When threatened with the death penalty for praying to God, Daniel rejects the silence that would free him. He continues to pray, very possibly praying words from a precursor to the Amidah.[47]

He seeks the Kingdom first and trusts in God's principle. Thrown into a den of lions, he is provided with what he needs—an angel to rescue him.

cheek

Application #5: *Seek first, and your actions will speak louder than words.*

Thirty years ago I protected a young boy at school by turning the other cheek.

It was fractured in three places.

My classmates had often taunted me for my faith and questioned my commitment. They even invented a game called 'crucify the Christian' to badger me when teachers were absent. A common accusation was that I would not really do what

Christians were supposed to do, and in a school where violence was prevalent, turning the other cheek was given as an example.

After the incident where I actually fulfilled Jesus' command, the bully had threatened to attack me again. A time and date were set.

But he never showed up. In fact, I never saw him again!

It turned out that my entire class hunted him down. A group of lads told him:

> "Paul Gibbs is a Christian. Mess with him and you mess with the Sixth Form."

Soon the boy transferred to another school.

I never discovered what happened until years later when I bumped into one of my old classmates. He had apparently decided to follow Jesus, and when I turned up to speak at his church, he told me the story of what he and my fellow students had done.

I learned then that we can speak or we can seek first.

One fulfills a duty; the other advances the Kingdom.

ideas to consider

Picture this Kingdom Principle as the foundation of your world.

In the exercise of this chapter, you imagined everything in your local community happening just as things would happen in heaven. What visual images came to mind? How did you picture Jesus' command to love God and love one another displayed at your local Wal-Mart? What footage did you see when you visualized His grace and mercy dominating your local neighborhood? What scenarios played out as you envisioned His level of honesty, integrity, and ethics in your work place?

How must your own behavior change to help make this vision a reality?

Write your thoughts in the cloud below.

KINGDOM PRINCIPLE 2 ✢ JUDGE AND BE JUDGED

2

I vow to show mercy and grace to the King's children,
knowing the King Himself will show grace and mercy to me.

W.C.

Humor arises from many types of circumstances.

From observation. From awkwardness. From farce.

But more often than not, the greatest humor comes from misunderstanding.

A story I used to use when teaching in schools was about an English lady planning a vacation to Germany during the early 20th century—a time period when you could not assume indoor plumbing was available. Prior to her visit, the lady sent a letter, requesting details of the bathroom, to the German schoolmaster whose home she was renting.

Rather than using the word 'toilet,' she asked him for specifics about the W.C. which in England represents the water closet and is a polite way of referring to the place we do our private business.

Unfortunately, the abbreviation was unknown to the German schoolteacher who immediately contacted the most knowledgeable person in the village, the local church minister. Together they decided that it must refer to a wayside chapel.

And so, the story goes that he sent her the following reply:

> *Dear Madam,*
>
> *I take great pleasure in informing you that the W.C. is located nine miles from the house, nestled in a lovely grove of pine trees. It is capable of holding two hundred and twenty-nine people and is open on Sundays and Thursdays. As there are many people expected in the summer months, I suggest you arrive early. There is, however, plenty of standing room. This is an unfortunate situation, especially if you are in the habit of going regularly. It may be of some interest to you that my daughter was married in the W.C. In fact, it was there that she met her husband. It was a blessed event. There were ten people for every seat. It was wonderful to see the expressions on their faces.*

My wife, sadly, has been ill and unable to go recently. It has been almost a year since she went last, which pains her greatly. You will be pleased to know that many people bring their lunch and make a day of it. Others prefer to wait until the last minute and arrive just in time! I would recommend your ladyship plan to go on a Thursday, as there is an organ accompaniment. The acoustics are excellent and even the most delicate sounds can be heard everywhere. The newest addition is a bell that chimes a lovely melody at the time of release.

I look forward to escorting you there myself, and seating you in a place where you can be seen by all.

With deepest regards,
The Schoolmaster

Misunderstandings are a great source for comedians.

But more often than not, misunderstandings lead to frustration and anger, as well as bitterness, embarrassment, and hurt. Perhaps the most destructive result of misunderstanding comes when we judge people wrongly.

When that is the case, the result is anything but funny.

613

When I was a small boy, walking along the seaside pier provided simple entertainment during family holidays. The wooden cutouts there created all kinds of merriment. These painted caricatures, with holes where faces should have been, commonly featured stereotypes such as skinny old men, bikini-clad girls, or overweight, jolly, middle-aged women.

The fun came when you put your face in the gap and took photographs. The greatest mismatch always produced the biggest laughs.

My Grandpops, for instance, would put his seventy-year-old face in the head of a muscular lifeguard and ask, "What's so funny?"

Sadly, seaside cutouts give insight into why the Church can also become a laughing stock . . .

The body does not match the head.

The Church is the body of Christ. Jesus is its head.

The bigger the mismatch, the more foolish it seems.

And here lies the problem.

God's dream has been to create a community that takes care of itself through a system of human *responsibilities*.

Instead, our dream has been to create a community that takes care of itself through a system of human *rights*.

Human rights versus human responsibilities.

Have we individualized the gospel message so much that we miss the point of how Jesus intended it to spread?

Have we lost a key principle, causing the world to take us far less seriously than it should?

According to the tradition of Jesus' religion, God gave 613 commandments in the Torah. What is interesting about this number is that a hint is hidden within it. There is a clue to a hidden meaning and a deeper truth.

Of the 613 commands, 248 are positive [things to do] and 365 are negative [things not to do]. This corresponds to the 248 bones and the 365 muscles of the human body categorized by the Talmud.[48]

There is intimation here.

The key to abundant life concerns a body not an individual.

What is revolutionary is this—it is physically impossible for one person to obey all 613 commands.

To fulfill some, you have to be a priest.
To fulfill others, you must be a man.
To fulfill still others, you must be female.
A few can be only obeyed when living in the land of Israel.

In other words, the only way Israel could be saved was in community!

Here is a hidden sign, at one point concealed, but intended to be disclosed.

If we miss His context, we miss His point.

Jesus' parables describe a community that seeks first His Kingdom by putting others first. This is His method of displaying God's love to the world.

In the mind of Jesus, an individual cannot display the Kingdom of God *alone*.

plural

Jesus sent people out in teams.

Why? Because the connection between humans displays the Kingdom, not simply the humans themselves.

I think we have forgotten this vital fact because human rights dominate our culture. I can have a conversation with a Christian who thinks that Christianity is simply about his or her relationship with Jesus, his or her needs, his or her vision.

I can walk into a coffee shop and meet followers of Jesus who don't see a need for being a committed member of a church family because they can get teaching from YouTube and download worship from iTunes.

They have completely misunderstood the point of church. They have misinterpreted Jesus' teaching on the body. The way they have entered church has determined the way they have exited it. And exited many of them have.

When I lose sight of my relationships, I lose sight of the thing that grounds my religion. If I am to be a knight and help rescue the image of the Church, I must be willing to defeat a foe who has sought to pervert the nature of Christ's body.

To pervert: to divert to a wrong end or purpose.

Satan deceives people from one extreme to another. He either seeks to promote within us an *impersonal* religion or one where the *person* is the religion.

If we are transfixed upon the line, we become worshippers who are encouraged on Sundays to block out other people in order that we might concentrate on feeling God for ourselves. We possess a faith where we sow in order that *we* might receive. We follow a religion where *we* can own our very own *personal* Jesus.

And so, here is the problem we face:

> *What if we have not been trained to understand that our connection to God is deeply evident in our connection to one another?*
>
> *What if, when we fight for our individual rights, we fight against God's plan?*
>
> *What if we think we can break a promise to people without breaking a promise to God?*
>
> *What if our days of prayer and fasting, our dedication to the latest techniques, and our commitment to passion are undermined by an ignorance of a principle so very close to the King's heart?*
>
> *What if God will not partner with a group who judges each other for the wrong motives?*

The Spirit of God wrestles with a religion like that.

He promises *we* will overcome our enemy by the blood of the Lamb and the word of *our* testimony.[49]

Plural not singular.

Recently a young man, who had been caught up into a gang named 'The Wolf Pack,' shared how he had been attracted to a team of Pais members.

When interviewed and asked what had influenced him, he said that their language was cleaner and that there was:

". . . a light you could see in the eyes of all of them not just one of them." [50]

He emphasized *all*.

An individual can be unique, but a team demonstrates a pattern.

It is the testimony of a *body* of people, not an individual that will overcome our spiritual enemy.

sadducees

A.W. Tozer said that whatever drops into your mind when you think about God is singularly the most important thing about you. [51]

Why?

Because whoever you see God as, you will eventually become to other people.

For instance, the Pharisees saw God as a judge; therefore, they judged others.

Tozer was right. Believing in God is not the only important thing; it's the God you believe in that is crucial.

Repeatedly, we are warned about the religion of the Pharisees. I wonder though if the faith of the Sadducees is what we really need to watch out for. The Sadducees were the main enemy of Jesus, even more so than the Pharisees whose teaching—not actions—Jesus generally agreed with. [52]

Josephus, the Jewish historian, said the Sadducees did not emphasize God's interest in man's decisions. To them, God was not relational. And therefore, they favored religion over relationship.

They were a proud and unforgiving group of people. From the Jewish aristocracy, they looked down on anyone who did not have the same training as they did. They were lovers of religion and believers in God, but they were fixated upon the line, not the cloud.

Interestingly, Josephus also reported:

> . . . the behavior of the Sadducees one towards another is in some degree wild, and their conversation with those that are of their own party is as barbarous as if they were strangers to them . . .[53]

Being impersonal caused them to become impervious.

They resisted Jesus.

They resisted His parables because they resisted His plan.

transformation

Could we be in danger of missing God's plan as well?

Jesus came to bring a spiritual transformation that was never intended to simply transform the spirit. It was intended to transform the *world*.

But how would Jesus bring this transformation? Would it be through politics?

In the first book of the trilogy, I outlined the four main political and philosophical groups of Jesus' day.

> The Zealots hoped for a militaristic leader to set up a new world order by first overthrowing the Romans . . . but were disappointed by a Jesus who taught His disciples to carry their enemy's backpack an extra mile.

> The Sadducees were relatively happy to play church and ignore many of the issues of the day. They would have loved a Rabbi who preached the extra mile sermon and would not rock the boat . . . but they were threatened by a man who preached a new kind of kingdom.

> The Essenes rejected the general Jewish population as worldly and set up their own isolated new world order. Their philosophy of sharing and community, plus their commitment to a less materialistic lifestyle, had obviously influenced Jesus . . . but they were confused by a Messiah who engaged a city that they had discarded.

The Pharisees taught that if Israel first cleaned up its act and got rid of sin [i.e., the sinners], then God would send the Messiah. They thought they had hit the jackpot when Jesus told his talmidin to do what they taught . . . but were forever disgruntled when He forbid them to do as they did.

All four groups had a different political agenda and used their religion to push it.

Do you know why the early Church ceased to meet with the Jews in the synagogues? It is partly because, at the end of the first century, the Pharisees added into the eighteen benedictions of the Amidah a curse upon the followers of Jesus and the Samaritans.[54] Consequently, the disciples could no longer be connected to their Jewish brethren.

The Pharisees had successfully used their religion for their own personal gain.

So, can the Kingdom be political?

Yes. If the definition of politics is the way a society structures itself, then the disciples were not wrong to expect Jesus to bring a kingdom that was political.

They were wrong, however, in thinking His Kingdom would *come* through politics.

It would not come through politics or violence as the Zealots thought, or through the appeasement politics that the Sadducees propagated. It would not arrive by the separatist politics of the Essenes or the Pharisees' passive-aggressive system of religious politics.

It would come through a new command.

"A new command I give you: Love one another. As I have loved you, so you must love one another. By this all men will know that you are my disciples, if you love one another."[55]

A new command with a Kingdom Principle at its heart.

questions to ask

Have I individualized my religion?

Am I concerned about the reputation of God's body?

When it comes to being a part of the human race, what concerns me most?

My rights?

My responsibilities?

Am I demanding that God still use me but refusing to let anyone challenge me?

Would people describe me as a *consumer* or a *contributor?*

How have I experienced restoration and how have I offered it to . . .

a family member?

an enemy?

a colleague?

What one word comes to my mind when I hear the word *God?*

What kind of promises am I after?

What kind of treasure do I hope to gain?

If God's rewards for me impacted the community but not me, how would I feel?

Am I motivated by what motivates the King?

Do I resist acting on His parables because I ultimately am resisting His plan?

questions to add:

KINGDOM PRINCIPLE 2

JUDGE AND BE JUDGED ||THE PRINCIPLE

forgotten

At the beginning of the book, I asked the question, "Does God have favorites?"

I also asked why it is that two people can do similar things but seem to be treated differently in the Kingdom of God.

The closest we will ever get to a straight answer falls from the lips of Jesus.[56]

> *Do not judge, or you too will be judged. For in the same way you judge others, you will be judged, and with the measure you use, it will be measured to you.* (NIV)

> *Judge not, that ye be not judged. For with what judgment ye judge, ye shall be judged: and with what measure ye mete, it shall be measured to you again.* (KJV)

> *Stop judging others, and you will not be judged. For others will treat you as you treat them. Whatever the measure you use in judging others, it will be used to measure how you are judged.* (NLT)

> *For with the judgment you judge, you will be judged.* (Literal Greek)

If *Seek First* is the *foundational* principle, then *Judge and Be Judged* is the *forgotten* principle.

In His command, Jesus tells us that however we decide to treat others, God will treat us. How often do we hear that? Common preaching gives us six or seven steps to being blessed, and yet leaves us still missing much of the point: Our relationship with one another has a deep impact on our relationship with God.

We sometimes forget this principle, perhaps hoping God will forget it also.

We may even challenge the concept. It has been done before . . .

> *"Am I my brother's keeper?"*[57]

God does not forget, however, and neither should we.

calculator

Is a calculator really what God had in mind?

If Jesus is correct, the Father is not in heaven meticulously moving beads to and fro on some ancient abacus.

He is not adding up our misdemeanors and comparing them with the sins of others. He is not looking to cream off the top percentage of rule keepers, those whose moral grade point average takes them to the head of the class.

He is not interested in *comparing* us with each other but rather in *connecting* us with each other.

When it comes to living life, cloud-dwellers are challenged by *His* questions:

> *Will you first take the plank out of your own eye?*
> *Will you compare yourself to Me and not to him or her?*
> *Will you be the first to drop the stone, not the first to throw it?*

However, line-dwellers challenge God by *their* questions:

> *How much should I forgive?*
> *Why should I forgive?*
> *What should I forgive?*

We struggle with this Kingdom Principle perhaps more than any other.

We bring our stories of what was done to us. We work out what *we* did, we work out what *they* did, and we work to compare them. We work out who is right, and we work out who is wrong. We work out whether we should forgive, and we work out what we are entitled to begrudge.

That's a lot of work!

But I do not believe that our Creator is interested in pluses and minuses, multiplication or division, when it comes to relationships. Jesus came to bring an understanding of the Father's heart so we can throw the calculator away.

Yet still, we compare ourselves.

"If I am better than he is," we think, "then I am okay with God."

If you want to know the heart of the King, it is not something you *work out*; it is something you *work in*.

Knights of this Kingdom Principle will swap the labels, throw out the calculator, and instead gain a spiritual compass.

compass

How might we understand this Kingdom Principle in terms of the cloud and the line? On one extreme of the line is vengeance, and on the other end is justice.

This was summed up in the Law of Moses:

". . . an eye for an eye, a tooth for a tooth."[58]

It is a command that may seem harsh at first sight (no pun intended). It may even appear cruel or vindictive, but let me try to explain what was going on by giving you a little context.

God's way is always that He meets us in our ignorance, holds our hand, and patiently brings us towards a better understanding of who He is and what He wants from and for us. In order to do this, He has made five covenants with mankind, each one bringing us a little closer to the kind of relationship He desires. The covenants were formed with Noah, Abraham, Moses, David, and Jesus.[59]

In each of these key moments in history, the King renegotiated His relationship with His servants. Each covenant produced a more fully developed follower. Starting with Noah who was 'relatively righteous,' they lead to the disciples of Jesus whom the Son of God referred to as *friends*. Why? Because they were given understanding.[60, 61]

As the Bible recounts, before the Law of Moses, vengeance ruled. For example, if a man were robbed and lost his eye in the fight, his brothers would take revenge by killing the thief. This was a long way from the heart of a King whose Kingdom is best modeled by a community of people who live according to His ways.

Then God introduced the Law of Moses and replaced vengeance with justice. Suddenly there was a restriction. If that man's eye comes out, the brothers may no longer seek the death penalty but only reparation. Eventually, a whole legal system was introduced into the Jewish world, mainly involving monetary compensation for a whole litany of outlined offenses.

It would appear that justice is the way to go. Justice requires working things out, finding out what is *fair*.

But is our definition of *justice* really what is in God's heart?

No, there is something much more. There is the cloud, and in the cloud, you don't find vengeance or even simple justice.

You find *grace*.

A natural compass points to true north; the spiritual compass points to true grace.

There is a paradox here. Grace cannot be earned, yet because we show grace, even more is given to us. It does not seem to make sense, but in the Kingdom of God all things are possible.

Grace causes us to go the extra mile, and only when we go the extra mile is the Kingdom of God advanced.

Grace *is* the extra mile.

forward

Jesus was very keen to teach grace and this forgotten Kingdom Principle. To illustrate the point, He even made up a story.[62] The tale is about a servant who is forgiven a huge debt by a king. But when the servant refuses to forgive a debt that is owed to him, the king finds out and changes his mind. He punishes the servant, telling him:

> *"I canceled all that debt of yours because you begged me to. Shouldn't*
> *you have had mercy on your fellow servant just as I had on you?"*[63]

Jesus' parable gives us greater insight into the heart of God than many of the factual stories of the Old Testament.

It moves us forward.

Let me explain by comparing it to a passage that Jesus' audience would have been familiar with.

As recorded in 2 Samuel 11, King David steals another man's wife, impregnates her, and then plots her husband's death. The prophet Nathan shows up and tells the king a story about a rich man who steals a humble peasant's only sheep.[64]

When David reacts with no mercy for the rich man, demanding harsh punishment for the thief, Nathan reveals that David is the rich man in the story. The prophet then pronounces judgment on David in the same fashion that David passed judgment on the fictitious thief.

David demanded death, and death is the result—the death of his son.

The story of David and Nathan poses a question:

> *If David had reacted differently to the story, would God's judgment have*
> *been modified?*

Jesus' parable of the unmerciful servant may help us decide.

Notice the difference in Jesus' fictitious story and the historic retelling of David's partial downfall.

Do you see it?

In the Old Testament stories, we often have no idea how God would have treated the perpetrator until the final judgment was passed. But in this parable, we do.

It gives us insight.

The king was going to forgive the servant his debt—a full pardon. But in the parable, the character that represented God actually changed his mind.

Or you might say, he had his mind changed for him.

Jesus' point was not that God is fickle, but that the Jews had lost something in their understanding of their Father.

Jesus was reminding His audience of the forgotten principle.

armor

Rarely is it our Bible knowledge, theology, gifts, vision, or devotional life that Jesus uses to determine our relationship with Him. It is how seriously we keep our promise to Him through our covenant relationship with others.

Do we really understand this? I don't think I used to.

In the late eighties, when I was training with a missionary organization, I made lots of friends. Two of my favorite people were very different indeed.

Gary had been a male prostitute on the streets of London and was going through a discipleship training school in order to work out the junk of his life and practice his newly acquired salvation. Frank was European, deeply religious, a long-term follower, and what I then considered to be very spiritual.

I enjoyed the company of both of them, but Frank and Gary just never got along.

I think Gary may have been a little intimidated by Frank who spent two hours very early each morning praying in isolation and memorizing scriptures that he seemed to know back to front. Frank was certainly offended by Gary's rough and ready demeanor. "Gaz," as I called him, had not yet fully understood the etiquette of being a Christian. Years of sexual abuse as a child and banishment—being stuffed into a locked closet for hours—had taken its toll on him.

In the last week of our course, at a special party, Gary approached Frank in the hope of making amends. He told him that he was sorry that they had not gotten along better, but wanted to assure him that he wished him all the best and would be praying for him over the coming months.

A few hours later, Gary ran into our dormitory, shaking from head to foot, crying because he had messed up. It turns out that Frank had complained to the leaders that, when Gary approached him, he had patted him on the back. In Frank's mind, this was a spiritual attack—a place where there was no spiritual armor.[65]

So tell me, who held the most promise—the ex-prostitute or the super-spiritual Bible student?

The answer is . . . both of them.

But perhaps Frank was in danger of wasting a life dedicated to knowing God's Word, but not understanding it.

family

How can we know God's Word but not understand it?

Again . . . if we miss its context.

The Kingdom Principle *Judge and Be Judged* can only be fully understood and embraced when we realize it lies within a greater truth:

> *Christ sees our commitment to Christ through our commitment to the body of Christ.*

Lynn and I are blessed with two incredible sons, Joel and Levi. I love my family more than anything in the world!

But do they sometimes embarrass me? Of course they do.

Do they sometimes let me down? Of course they do.

Now imagine one day I am speaking at a conference and a delegate comes up to me afterwards. He tells me how much he loved my talk and how convinced he is that we could be good friends. He offers to take me out to lunch, but first wants to mention that he thinks my wife is annoying and my kids are brats. After doing this, he says that he hopes this will not affect our relationship, and then he asks for a hug.

Be assured, he will get a physical response, but it may not be the one he was looking for.

Of course, this is a ridiculous and hypothetical situation . . . or is it?

Is this not exactly what worship leaders throughout the western world say on a Sunday morning?

> *"Just block out the people around you and focus on Jesus."*

No! The entire point of church is to do just the opposite.

We must focus on others *as* we focus on Jesus.

We can have that alone time with God at any point during the week that we deem it worth the time to create. Church, however, was shaped for the purpose of coming together and bringing what little we have and throwing it into the corporate pot.

pot

The only story I remember from religious assemblies at school was of three homeless people. Each man huddled around a fire with one item of food. One had a potato, the other a carrot, and the third a piece of meat. They decided that for the common good, to make the meal healthier and more interesting, they would all throw their contribution into a pan of boiling hot water to make a stew.

But in the dark, as the pan was passed around, each man decided to withhold his gift for himself, thinking that no one would notice.

As the story continued, the three men put their spoons into a pan that simply contained water. Lifting the spoons to their lips with hidden embarrassment, each man spoke the word, "Tasty!" All three carried on "eating," unable to point the finger because they knew they had each committed the same sin.

For too many, this is church.

We have missed the point.

> *Instead, be filled with the Spirit, speaking to one another with psalms, hymns, and songs from the Spirit.*[66]

We should come together for the purpose of being Jesus to each other. As we do so, He will pour back more of the same that we have just poured out.

Church becomes alive, organic, fresh!

challenge

Please understand that forgetting this principle can seriously damage our spiritual health. We cannot continue ignoring something so crucial to the Father in the way that He deals with you and me.

This wider principle is not an isolated thought. Consider the following:

> *. . . for the sake of his body which is the church.*[67]

> *Religion that God our Father accepts as pure and faultless is this: to look after orphans and widows in their distress . . .*[68]

> *"Then the righteous will answer him, 'Lord, when did we see you hungry and feed you, or thirsty and give you something to drink? When did we see you a stranger and invite you in, or needing clothes and clothe you? When did we see you sick or in prison and go to visit you?' The King will reply, 'I tell you the truth, whatever you did for one of the least of these brothers of mine, you did for me.'"*[69]

> *"For if you forgive other people when they sin against you, your heavenly Father will also forgive you. But if you do not forgive others their sins, your Father will not forgive your sins."*[70]

These truths convey a general rule that you cannot have a great relationship with God and a terrible one with everyone else.

Whoever claims to love God yet hates a brother or sister is a liar. For whoever does not love their brother and sister, whom they have seen, cannot love God, whom they have not seen.[71]

Why do we think we can hold resentment and bitterness toward others, show a poor commitment to the body of Christ, and yet want the opportunity to use our talents for His purposes?

Are you the kind of person desperate to make a difference but feel like you are going around in circles?

Can you be honest with yourself . . .

Could it be that you have no spiritual root? Could it be that you have jumped out of one relationship with God's people after another? Are you demanding that God still use you but refusing to let anyone challenge you?

Could you, in fact, be challenging God?

things to learn

The Jews recognized 613 commandments, and this hinted at God's body.

Christ sees my commitment to Him through my commitment to His people.

God is not interested in *comparing* me with others but *connecting* me with them.

The King is very interested in how and why I judge others.

However I decide to treat others, God will treat me.

Jesus' parables show that the King chooses to forgive me the way I forgive others.

If I ignore His principle, I am challenging Him.

The heart of the King isn't something to *work out* but something to *work in*.

In the cloud, you don't find vengeance or even simple justice. You find grace.

Grace *is* the extra mile.

The entire point of church is to focus on others as we focus on Jesus.

additional notes:

motive

Question: Can you imagine a community like this?

A life where a son betrays a father, but he is not just forgiven and then treated with caution and suspicion. Instead, he is trusted with his father's business.

A life where a wife betrays a husband, but she is not simply forgiven and then emotionally held at arm's length. She is restored to an even deeper and intimate friendship.

A life where a thief steals from a wealthy man, but he is not simply forgiven and then banned from the premises. He is given a job.

How full would that life be?

How might God's Kingdom be advanced if we pushed past vengeance and went beyond simple justice to model grace, trusting our powerful King to restore what we have lost?

And if grace is the key, why is it sometimes okay to judge but sometimes it is not?

In our lives, judgment is often expressed as a form of wisdom. We are commanded to discern all manner of issues in other people such as sin, heresy, those we should follow, and those we should not, and even the people we choose to call friends.

> *Bad company corrupts good character.*[72]

Judging in itself is not only permitted; it is encouraged.

Jesus was not addressing the *action* of judging but how and why we do it.

Knights of the Kingdom Principles understand that the most important judgment in life is to judge their own hearts.

We have to ask ourselves *why*.

Why are we judging? Why are we so keen to judge?

When we judge our own hearts first, we will be rewarded with the positive side of the principle. The Kingdom Principle *Judge and Be Judged* carries many promises for us. Each one can lead us to expect great things.

kebob

Expectation #1: *Judge with grace, and you will have the King for a friend.*

First, we must commit to the process by being honest with ourselves.

Could it be that you judge others in order to divert attention from yourself?

Is this not exactly what Adam did when he sinned? He blamed Eve and even God.[73] It seems that we judge others in the mistaken belief that, when conviction comes, attack is the best form of defense.

Could it be that your judgments spring from your own pain?

The old saying is true: *Hurt people hurt people.* Some people allow a stab in the back to protrude through their front. They are prickly people. Overly sensitive, yet insensitive to others, they stab everyone they come in contact with. Hurt people attract and connect with others. They create a 'hurt kebob.'

Could it be that you don't really want to be free from the hurt in your life?

Perhaps it gets you the attention you so desperately feel you need. For instance, a little boy once said with a big smile on his face, "Mummy, today, I have decided to be sad." Puzzled, his mother immediately asked why. He explained, "Because when you are sad, the teacher gives you a hug." That is cute when you are three, but not when you are thirty-three.

Are you harboring your hurt?

A harbor serves a special purpose. We bring our boats there for protection from strong winds. Have you noticed that the Holy Spirit has often been described as a wind? Are you protecting your hurt from His Spirit?

Could it be that you feel superior to others when you judge them?

Whatever the reason, we must understand that as we judge, we will be judged. In the way that we judge, we will be judged. And for the reason we judge, we will be judged.

Yet as we allow the Holy Spirit to finally deal with these things, we will not simply be set free from the negative side of this principle, but we will also receive the promises of the positive side. We will be made pure.

> *"One who loves a pure heart and who speaks with grace will have the king for a friend."*[74]

Perhaps this is the greatest promise of all!

ammunition

Expectation #2: *Judge with grace, and God will have your back.*

Our judgment of others not only hurts us, but hurts those who come in contact with us. As I wrote in my last book:

> *When bull elephants fight, the grass always loses.*[75]

If we love His wider purposes, we will not lash out at others because we may do them harm. God is building His Church, and as He does so, our role is to take on His new commandment.

> *"A new command I give you: Love one another. As I have loved you, so you must love one another."*

When we do this, He keeps His promise:

> *For the LORD will vindicate his people and have compassion on his servants.*[76]

It is God's job to prove you right. It is His responsibility to argue your case. You have to decide now if you trust Him to do it.

Trusting Him requires an act of omission. We omit our right to fight.

This does not make us pushovers. It did not make Jesus one either. Our response is not that we do nothing; it is that we do not seek to cause harm to others in order to protect ourselves.

We are not to become *passive;* we are to become *partners.*

We partner with God by doing our utmost to show integrity, honesty, and commitment. We stick to our guns, but we do it with genuine kindness and grace. As we do this, we provide ammunition for God as He fights on our behalf to prove us right.

To emphasize this point, Paul quotes the Hebrew Tanakh with its usual graphic word pictures and hyperbole:

> *If your enemy is hungry, feed him; if he is thirsty, give him something to drink. In doing this, you will heap burning coals on his head. Do not be overcome by evil, but overcome evil with good.*[77]

To retaliate is to hand the initiative over to my enemy who will provoke us into a game of *tit* for *tat.*

> *Put on the full armor of God, so that you can take your stand against the devil's schemes.*[78]

To trust is to regain the initiative. It is to believe the promise that God has your back.

And we need Him to have our back.

> *For our struggle is not against flesh and blood, but against the rulers, against the authorities, against the powers of this dark world and against the spiritual forces of evil in the heavenly realms.*[79]

Grace is the stone that will slay your Goliath, and this Kingdom Principle is the sling from which to throw it.

agape

Expectation #3: *Judge with grace, and all men will know you belong to Him.*

Jesus promised:

> *"By this all men will know that you are my disciples, if you love one another."*[80]

By what exactly? By *love*?

Really? Everyone loves!

Yes, but by a different kind of love.

The Greek language has three main words for love.

One word is *eros* and is found in secular Greek literature. Eros is human love and often refers to sensual love.

In high school, I worked part-time in retail. One day over 2,000 Mills & Boon books were delivered, and my job was to stack them in order. These romantic novels were really popular at the time with young girls that I knew, and so, intrigued, I checked them out over my lunch breaks that week. I discovered that they all had various titles such as:

> *The Millionaire's Misbehaving Mistress*
> *The Untamed Sheik*
> *Blackmailed Into the Billionaire's Bed*
> *Snowed in with the Boss*

But they all had the same story!

The heroine would be called something like Josephine or Jezebel. She was feminine, delicate, and feisty all rolled into one. Then she would meet *him*: Butch or Dirk. He might be a pilot, he might be a gardener, or he might be a doctor. But he was always a *beast*! She hated him. He was loathsome, he was arrogant, he was out of control . . . but there was just something about him.

About two-thirds into the book (I could almost guess the page number), there would be *the incident*. Maybe they were on a train that jerked and they would bump into each other. Or maybe she fell off a horse and he would catch her. He would lean forward to kiss her. She would resist, but ultimately, she just couldn't.

Mills & Boon books were about *eros* love. They were soppy, they were cheesy, and in those days at least, they were fairly innocent.

Eros love says, "I love you because you make me feel good."

(And while you make me feel good, I will continue to love you.)

Philo love is a higher level of love that concentrates on *our* happiness rather than simply *my* happiness. Philo is love's halfway mark. It gives a little and gets a little. It is a fifty-fifty proposition.

Philo love says, "I love you, because together we feel good."

(And while we feel good, I will continue to love you.)

Agape love is the highest level of love. It does not seek pleasure for itself, but instead delights in giving. It is not ignited by the merit or worth of the object of its affection. It is sparked by its own God-given nature.

God is agape.

Agape love says, "I love you because God loved me first."

(And because God loves me always, I will always love you.)

Jesus is referring to agape when He tells us that all men will know we are His disciples by our love. It is not our Christian title that will mark us.

People don't read titles. They read traits.

How would you read this sign posted at the gate of a convent?

> *Private property, absolutely no trespassing - Violators will be prosecuted to the full extent of the law! - Signed the Sisters of Mercy*

Jesus is calling out to you. He is asking if you can love others simply because you have already been loved by Him. Jesus is calling you from line-dwelling to cloud-dwelling. He is leading us by the hand from vengeance through justice to grace.

His love keeps moving us on.

As we grow in love, He promises we will grow in reputation as His disciples.

But remember, Jesus also promised that how they treated Him they will treat us. Make your pursuit His glory because it may not lead to yours.

gods

Expectation #4: *Judge with grace, and you will prove Jesus is God.*

When Jesus said, *"By this all men will know that you are my disciples,"* He was promising something special to us.

We, like all of His creation, can prove His existence.

In Jesus' time, there were many gods with many disciples.

The god Mithra was said to have come to earth six hundred years before Christ. Born in a cave to a virgin, he was worshiped by shepherds and had twelve follow-ers. The faithful referred to Mithra as "the light of the world" and celebrated his birth on December 25th.

Adis, who was worshiped from 200 BC, was hung on a tree and several days later was said to have rose from the dead. Adis was also thought to be born of a virgin.

Adonis was from around the same time as Jesus, was referred to as the son of God, born of a virgin, and said to have died to save mankind.

Horus was a much older Egyptian god, but was worshiped by some in Jesus' region. Horus died by crucifixion, and it was said that, as a small child, foreign kings had brought him gifts.

When Julius Caesar died, a comet was reported as having being seen by twelve witnesses. His followers testified that it was a sign of him rising from the dead and ascending to the right hand of the gods.

When Caesar Augustus lived, a twelve-day celebration of his birth was instigated. It was given the title 'Advent.' In the days of Romans, popular slogans were *"Caesar is lord"* and *"There is no other name under heaven by which man can be saved than that of Caesar."*

Our titles, our slogans, and even many of our beliefs are not that unique. But while other gods have been disproved and passed into history, the conviction that Jesus is alive has grown.

Why? Because by our agape for one another, He has proven His reality.

This supernatural power called agape realigns people's value and turns them upside down. Nothing on the planet has had such power to change so many.

This agape love transformed the way entire communities behaved. In the society in which Jesus was born, Roman citizens were more protected than non-citizens. Men were more privileged than women, and masters were higher than slaves. And yet, one of Jesus' followers observed that in a Jesus community . . .

> *"There is neither Jew nor Gentile, neither slave nor free, nor is there male and female, for you are all one in Christ Jesus."*[81]

Agape will turn your world upside down, and this Kingdom Principle will help you prove your God is all you say He is.

knots

Expectation #5: *Judge with grace, and you will have the power to be restored.*

Not only that, but you will inherit the power to restore others.

> *"If you forgive anyone's sins, their sins are forgiven; if you do not forgive them, they are not forgiven."*[82]

It took the disciples a long time to understand just what Jesus was talking about here. In fact, by the end of three years of being with Him, the value of agape and the Kingdom Principle *Judge and Be Judged* were not yet a part of their culture.

When Jesus was arrested and betrayed, His disciple Peter drew his sword and struck the servant of the high priest, cutting off his ear. The victim was the *Segine Hacohanim*, the chief priest's assistant.

The fact that his ear was cut off is significant. Cutting of an ear, specifically the earlobe, was often practiced because it automatically disqualified the servant from service in the Temple.[83] If the ear remained unhealed, then Peter would have succeeded in taking away not just his hearing but the servant's ability to serve God in his calling.

Peter did it on purpose. Yet, Jesus purposely healed him.

Jesus restored His enemy to a place of service to the Father.

Knights must not only be willing to *forgive*, but to go the extra mile and *restore*. Forgiving others is only a halfway step to this Kingdom Principle.

An object lesson I often use involves a piece of string with one end held high. At the top is a card with the word 'God,' and at the bottom, one with the word 'Man.' When we sin, it *feels* like a pair of scissors have cut the string and the relationship. The Father's style of forgiveness and restoration is like someone connecting the two ends of the string again—not with glue, but by tying a knot. If you glued them together, the distance between 'God' and 'Man' would be the same. By tying them back together with a knot, however, the two cards are closer than they were before.[84]

That's how I have felt in the past when I have sinned and God has forgiven me.

Closer.

Forgiveness maintains the Kingdom. Restoration advances it.

ideas to consider

Picture what life would look like if you never forgot this principle.

What if you were the first one to take the plank out of your own eye in your workplace, and in your neighborhood, the first to drop the stone rather than pick it up. Imagine yourself forgetting the hurts you have received from others and inspiring your children to do the same. See yourself as part of a church that performs acts of social grace rather than social justice. Imagine serving a community that brings people closer to each other in order to bring them closer to God, a life lived not by vengeance or justice but by grace.

What perpetrations do you need to forget when you remember this principle?

Give them to God by writing those things in the cloud below.

KINGDOM PRINCIPLE 3 ✧ RUBBISH IN RUBBISH OUT

3

I vow to be wise in the things my eyes see, ears hear, and heart joins,
knowing that the dragon will then be slain.

dragon

There is a dragon to slay.

> *The great dragon was hurled down—that ancient serpent called the devil,*
> *or Satan, who leads the whole world astray. He was hurled to the earth,*
> *and his angels with him.*[85]

No matter what our hopes and visions may be, unless we protect ourselves from our enemy, we can never be the hero we see in our dreams.

The English flag is the flag of Saint George, a red cross on a white background. It is the flag worn with pride across the chests of the English knights of history. The inspirational statue of Saint George and the dragon stands outside of Saint John's Wood Church in London where I was christened as a child. Our hero was a legendary knight who rescued villages from a monster that terrorized its inhabitants. Established in 1277, the cross of Saint George is one of the earliest known emblems representing my country, and in the thirteenth century, Saint George became the patron saint of England.

Knights inspire us!

Something happens to me when I see my flag waved at a sporting event.[86]

Something happens to me as I walk down the street and see it hanging from the window of every house in England during the World Cup.

Something happens to me when I see it raised on a flag pole during my national anthem.

The something that happens is an emotional, almost spiritual connection with my fellow patriots as we feel a surge of corporate strength and pride. It reminds us of our heritage, of our history, and of our heroes.

I want to be like Saint George, a knight who inspires others as they march into their own crusade toward personal holiness.

Don't you?

bath

I am embarrassed to admit it, but sometimes the way I relax is by having a bubble bath and lighting candles. I know it is awkward, but it's true. When my second son Levi was very young, he decided, for some reason only understood by him, that my 'spa time' was his opportunity to bond with his dad. As soon as I would escape to a hot bath, light the candles, and lie back, trying to think of nothing at all, Levi would walk in, sit down, and decide to have a chat while doing his 'ablutions.'

I wouldn't have minded so much, but he always insisted on giving me a running commentary. He also liked to ask me questions, and one day he asked me one of life's biggest puzzles:

> "Dad, what is the meaning of life?"

After I had tried my best to summarize my thoughts in a way that a three-year-old could understand, Levi was obviously still confused.

> "No, Dad," he said finally. "What is the meaning of *wife?*"

For a brief moment, I considered telling him it was an acronym for 'Washing, Ironing, Food, and Entertainment,' but then backed out of it when I processed the odds of him telling his mother.

My point is that sometimes, when all we want to do is relax and sit back, God asks us the toughest questions. And here is one I would like to pass on to you:

Is there power in your religion?

> *People will be lovers of themselves . . . having a form of godliness but denying its power.*[87]

Knights come in all shapes and sizes.

One of my favorite heroes is a man called Smith Wigglesworth, a once illiterate butcher, who became a kind of spiritual giant and motivated many to follow God and His Kingdom.

My favorite story of Wigglesworth is not the most dramatic, but it is the most quirky. The story goes that one day he boarded a train in England and simply sat opposite a man who was reading the newspaper. Wigglesworth, it is said, sat quietly in the six-person carriage looking aimlessly out the window when, after five minutes, the gentleman opposite threw down his newspaper and shouted:

"Okay, I can't stand it anymore! What must I do to be saved?"

I wish I could do that.

But sadly, I cannot. Like most of us, I am in pursuit of holiness. My journey sometimes feels like two steps forward and one step back but has best been described by one Biblical author in the form of a tongue twister:

> I do not understand what I do. For what I want to do I do not do, but what I hate I do. And if I do what I do not want to do, I agree that the law is good. As it is, it is no longer I myself who do it, but it is sin living in me. I know that nothing good lives in me, that is, in my sinful nature. For I have the desire to do what is good, but I cannot carry it out. For what I do is not the good I want to do; no, the evil I do not want to do—this I keep on doing. Now if I do what I do not want to do, it is no longer I who do it, but it is sin living in me that does it.[88]

I want to be a knight, but sometimes I feel more like the dragon.

I have to ask myself if I am really the inspiration to others that I want to be. If not, then what can I do about it?

limp

One of the problems I have in my quest to raise up young missionaries is the response so many of us have to the message of grace. It is as though grace has become an excuse for sin.

I wonder if the problem lies in the fact that when we think of our sin, we only contemplate its damage to our personal lives rather than to the Kingdom of God.

Our sin affects much more than just us.

It is better not to sin than to sin and be forgiven. Or, to paraphrase an old American preacher, if a man gets drunk and breaks his leg, God will indeed forgive him if he asks it, but he will always walk with a limp.[89]

Yes, you can sleep with your boyfriend, repent, and be forgiven, but you will no longer be a virgin.

Yes, you can commit adultery, repent, and be forgiven, but you may never command respect again.

Yes, you may commit fraud, repent, and be forgiven, but you will probably still do time in prison.

Is our teaching generating a people who want to be saved from hell but not from sin? A people who may be precious to God but not strategic?

When the Church goes the extra mile, the dragon gets worried. But if we are bound by our sin and regret, then we will not push forward. It is very difficult to run the good race when you are limping.

Our enemy knows that. He has a tactic to slow us down. Maybe even to stop us.

bungee

The devil doesn't know who you are.

God is omnipresent, but Satan is not.

I once had a pastor tell me that, as they prayed for their church building, he and his elders sensed that Lucifer had been in their restroom. He made an effort to ensure me that he didn't mean demons, but Lucifer himself.

I don't think so.

Maybe, just maybe, at that time, if Satan were wandering the planet, he might have visited Uganda, the Middle East, or Northern Ireland. But the toilets of a church in North Manchester?

I think not.

I don't think the devil has a clue who I am, nor do I believe he has any special plan or purpose that is unique to me.

> *No temptation has seized you except that which is common to man.*[90]

The dragon has a pattern, and it's not personal.

The dragon has a tactic, but it's not what you think.

First, he *tempts* us.

A common trick of our enemy is to deceive us into thinking that our problems are exclusive. We hear that others have faced sexual temptation, but we say to ourselves that no one has dealt with our *unique* situation. We understand that others have faced the challenges of greed, but we fool ourselves into thinking that no one has the *distinctive* needs that we have.

It is simply not true. Even Jesus was tempted with the same temptations that you and I face.

> *For we do not have a high priest who is unable to sympathize with our weaknesses, but we have one who has been tempted in every way, just as we are—yet was without sin.*[91]

The process of temptation is perhaps best illustrated by one of the wonders of the world. The Great Wall of China is approximately thirty feet high, eighteen feet thick, and 1,500 miles long. It was built to secure its nations borders, but within a hundred years, three armies had successfully broken through it.

They did not climb over it, smash through it, or walk around it.

They simply bribed the gatekeepers.[92]

All Satan is looking for is an Achilles' heel, an opportunity to turn a foothold into a stronghold. This is our enemy's *modus operandi*, the generic default setting he uses with every one of us.

Secondly, he *taunts* us.

After first saying, "It's okay, your situation is special," and "Don't worry, God will always forgive you," the split second we succumb, he turns around and attacks us for what we have just done. How can you possibly share your faith, he asks, when you just did, said, or watched that?

The devil is a title not a name.

Barack Obama is a name; the president of the United States is a title.

Alex Ferguson is a name; manager of the world's greatest football team is a title.

Lucifer and Satan are names; the devil is a title.

It occurs thirty-five times in the New Testament and means 'the accuser.' Now, please note that it does not mean 'the tempter.' Although we think the dragon's greatest tactic is that he *tempts* us, it is in fact that he *taunts* us.

One of the most basic lessons a preacher learns is, when you make a mistake, don't try to dig yourself out. A colleague of mine once spoke at a large youth event. While building up steam, waving his finger and pointing at people, he explained God's love for his audience. He told them that God did not care if they were too fat or too thin, too tall or too small or, as he pointed to one young lady, had a face like a Russian shot-putter.

The trouble is, she unfortunately did.

Instead of moving on, he began to dig a bigger trench for himself by telling her that he thought she was pretty. The legend of that terrible night goes on to say that he turned on the lights and took a vote to try to encourage her.

The preacher knew, as we all do, that accusation is a terrible thing. And if our enemy can find that one weakness that he can keep going back to, you can be sure he will.

He is looking for that spiritual bungee rope in your life, and he will pull on it as often as he can.

nail

We must not settle for salvation.

The King is calling you to a higher purpose than simply being saved. He is calling you to be strategic!

We must not be so content that we are happy to compromise.

There is a story of a man who was asked to sell his old cabin in the mountains. In order to make a profit, he agreed to do so on one condition. The contract would allow him to still own the nail in the roof of the porch. The buyer agreed to the compromise, and a couple weeks after he moved in, the original owner hung a dead cat from the nail. The stench became so bad that the buyer eventually sold the house back to the original owner at a vastly reduced price.

> *"When an evil spirit comes out of a man, it goes through arid places seeking rest and does not find it. Then it says, 'I will return to the house I left.' When it arrives, it finds the house unoccupied, swept clean and put in order. Then it goes and takes with it seven other spirits more wicked than itself, and they go in and live there. And the final condition of that man is worse than the first. That is how it will be with this wicked generation."* [93]

You and I are no different. The devil's tactic is the same for us all. But because our enemy uses a common tactic, our God has empowered us with a common strategy to defeat him.

And when I say strategy, I mean a *principle*.

questions to ask

Who inspires me and what effect have they had on my life?

How do I want to be an inspiration to others?

Is there *power* in my religion?

Am I limping? And if so, what did I do to cause it?

Do I want to be saved from hell but not saved from sin?

How do I see the devil's tactic in my life?

What has done more damage to the Kingdom growing within me?

> *The tempting?*

> *The taunting?*

Am I deceived into thinking my temptation is unique, that I am a special case?

Have I settled for salvation?

What tactics for combating the devil am I using? Are they working?

What foothold does he have in my life that is becoming a stronghold?

How much do I believe God when He says I can be victorious?

Do I have hope that I can move forward?

questions to add:

RUBBISH IN RUBBISH OUT || THE PRINCIPLE

creed

No magic wand will instantly change us so we can defeat our foe.

God may fill us with His Spirit, but do not confuse this with some lucky supernatural zap that will instantly turn us into perfect people.

Instead, we work out our salvation.

Yet even that can be misunderstood. Modern Jews believe that doing good deeds will make you a good person. If you behave, you will eventually become. They even have a slogan:

> *Deed over Creed.*

But laws do not make us good.

In his book, *A Year of Living Biblically*, A. J. Jacobs pursues a better version of himself by attempting to obey as many of the 613 commandments his Jewish faith tells him to. And yet he learns a profound lesson from a wise and unnamed scholar in the form of the following e-mail:

> *It is through being in Christ and following Him that we become transformed. Unless one takes this step, one cannot be truly transformed. So, after your year is over, you will go back to being a man who finds purpose in weird projects and writing assignments. Becoming a follower of Jesus Christ is much more rewarding.*[94]

It is true. There is a reward—the reward of becoming who you were meant to be.

The hero. The knight. The dragon slayer.

weapon

To enable us to gain that reward, the King has a weapon—and it is not what you think.

It is not a magic wand but a Kingdom Principle.[95]

The good man brings good things out of the good stored up in him, and the evil man brings evil things out of the evil stored up in him. (NIV)

A good man out of the good treasure of the heart bringeth forth good things: and an evil man out of the evil treasure bringeth forth evils things. (KJV)

A good person produces good things from the treasury of a good heart, and an evil person produces evil things from the treasury of an evil heart. (NLT)

Good in, good out. Rubbish in, rubbish out.

The Kingdom Principle *Rubbish In, Rubbish Out* concerns that which we choose to store within ourselves. What flows from our hearts—whether purity, faith, and hope, or perversion, lies, and doubt—is the product of what we first take in.

I have a friend who is a prolific preacher. He brings great content every time he opens his mouth. And yet, it seems very easy for him to prepare his messages. I once asked him how he managed to be able to preach something new so often on such short notice.[96] His reply was simple:

"I read constantly so there is always something brewing!"

Disciples develop through discipline, not dreaming.

We cannot spend our lives fantasizing about a magic zap. We cannot waste away, hoping to win some spiritual lottery. There is no supernatural X-factor, and no ecclesiastical panel member will suddenly declare you a spiritual superstar.

If *Judge and Be Judged* is the *forgotten* principle, then *Rubbish In, Rubbish Out* is the *formative* principle.

God forms us over time, and we get to partner with Him as He does it.

This is exciting to me. Who I am is not left to chance. My character is not left to the whim of a fickle god. It's a win-win. I get to decide who I want to be, but I also get a partner who can coach and resource me.

I don't have to do this alone, and I don't have to worry about being too easily influenced. Instead I can train myself by investing in as many of the right influences that I can.

I *can* live above the line.

worldly

When I was young and in pursuit of holiness, I knew little of this Kingdom Principle, and so I lived on the line.

I only really understood the rules, and without knowing it, I had compromised who I could be for what I could or could not do.

In those days, church taught me that men could not wear earrings or dye their hair. Women had to wear hats, and it was considered a sin for them to wear make-up (which was odd, because personally, I thought it was a sin for some of them not to).

Some pastors were ingenious at coming up with short, sharp one-liners to protect their flock. One young lady wearing make-up was greeted by a pastor with the words, "I see you've had your fingers in the devil's jam pot."

It was a sin to go to the cinema, and to have a television was frowned upon. Some considered certain musical instruments to be worldly. The list goes on.

I sometimes wondered . . . who makes this stuff up?

Who decides what is *worldly*?

When arguing our case for what is right and wrong, the desire to fixate upon the line is never stronger than in the topic of morality.

When it comes to righteousness, line-dwellers are constrained by *their* questions.

> *Which movie rating is okay for me to watch? R, PG-13, or PG?*
> *How short can my skirt length be? Thigh high, knee high, or ankle high?*
> *How far can we go? Holding hands, kissing, or fondling?*

Cloud-dwellers, however, are compelled by *His* questions.

> *How much do you care about My reputation?*
> *How free do you want to be to pursue My dream?*
> *How much of My power do you want in your religion?*

Cloud-dwellers obey with the knowledge that how they behave does not simply reflect upon themselves.

They are not prisoners to the religious police.

They are not earning air miles for a trip to heaven.

For them, the rules are not a slide rule but a springboard from which to live above the line.

As one cloud-dweller aptly said:

> *"Worldliness is that which cools our affections towards God."*[97]

fruit

Notice the flexibility employed by Paul in his letter to the saints in Galatia.

> *The acts of the flesh are obvious: sexual immorality, impurity and debauchery; idolatry and witchcraft; hatred, discord, jealousy, fits of rage, selfish ambition, dissensions, factions and envy; drunkenness, orgies, and the like. I warn you, as I did before, that those who live like this will not inherit the kingdom of God.*[98]

You might have thought he would then encourage his readers to run to the other extreme of the line. We may have expected him to list opposite acts: *marriage, sexual purity, abstinence, and church attendance.*

But instead he goes to the cloud.

> *But the fruit of the Spirit is love, joy, peace, forbearance, kindness, goodness, faithfulness, gentleness and self-control. Against such things there is no law.*[99]

The ancient Jew is wrong; the answer is not a *law-led life* but a *Spirit-led life*.

The modern Jew is wrong; the answer is not *deed over creed* but *cloud over creed*.

God has a principle; the devil has a tactic.

And both are about process.

corinth

One city housed Christians who succumbed to the demonic process.

Corinth was a church full of possibilities. The city was built on an isthmus off the Sardonic Gulf and the Ionian Sea. More than just ideal for seaside visits, it was perfectly situated for trade and a busy center for travelers.

To fulfill the Great Commission, the church of Corinth did not need to go into all the world because all the world was coming to them.

It was a wealthy city. The church had the potential as it grew to sponsor all sorts of missionary work.

It was full of ready listeners. The culture of the city fostered new ideas. Men loved to talk and listen. Rather than football and cars, religion and philosophy were their favorite subjects. If you had something to share, they were all ears.

Potential . . . something we always have but rarely grasp.

Corinth unfortunately fell foul to the process of *tempting* and *taunting*.

Two of the city's major practices were idolatry and sexual immorality. The city was home to the temples of various Greek gods such as Apollo, Ascepius, and Aphrodite who was at one time served by over twelve temples with hundreds of temple prostitutes. Corinth's reputation for sexual perversion was legendary. To *Corinthianize* meant to practice sexually immorality.

The city was a slang word for wickedness!

As Paul's letters to the church progress, we see them trace the step-by-step process of *Rubbish In, Rubbish Out* as he pleads with them to repent.

Take a look at the following chronological snippets.

Step #1: Association

> *I have written you in my letter not to associate with sexually immoral people.*[100]

This could not be clearer.

Step #2: Attraction

> *Flee from sexual immorality.*[101]

Those they allowed to influence their lives were having a negative effect on them. Have you noticed that when someone sins, their first goal is get others involved? Perhaps to a sinner, a sin shared is a sin halved.

Step #3: Adolescence

> *Brothers, I could not address you as spiritual but as worldly—mere infants in Christ. I gave you milk, not solid food, for you were not yet ready for it.*[102]

Spiritual immaturity brings deafness.

The ears can hear, but the heart cannot.

Step #4: Arguments

> *You are still worldly. For since there is jealousy and quarrelling among you, are you not worldly? Are you not acting like mere men? For when one says, "I follow Paul," and another, "I follow Apollos," are you not mere men?*[103]

When people's faith erodes, they switch from prayer to politics. Eventually their political support is given to those who will tell them what they want to hear.

Step #5: Apostasy

> *For such men are false apostles, deceitful workmen, masquerading as apostles of Christ.*[104]

Overall, there was a delayed reaction. Paul apparently wrote four letters to the church at Corinth. Some scholars believe that the two in our Bibles are really number two and number four.

Four letters wrestling with a hardhearted people.

horizontal

Corinth's Christianity had been corrupted. Ours must not be.

Ours must be a pure religion. Ours must be passed on.

When I read of Jesus' chastisement of the Pharisees for travelling over land and sea to make their converts twice the child of hell as themselves, I have often looked back and worried about what kind of religion I actually passed on to the young people I reached in schools.

The root meaning of the word *religion* is:

> *'to tie or bind over again, to make more fast.'*[105]

Will their religion—their *connection* to God—be simply an impersonal relationship with Christianity rather than a personal relationship with Christ Himself?

I must do better than that. We must do better than that.

When I was growing up, it seemed most Christians I knew loved Jesus but were sometimes embarrassed by the Christian Church. Our programs were often under-resourced, our meetings were sometimes awkward, and our attitude reflected the statement, "Oh it'll do; it's just for the church."

Nowadays it seems, we have learned the importance of excellence and have excelled in making everything as relevant and fun as possible.

It may be true to say, however, that in the past we *loved the Head* and *put up with His body,* but now we *love the body* and *put up with its Head.*

We have churches packed with spectators—saved, but not strategic.

When a good friend and I discussed this thought, it occurred to him that at a recent baptism service where he is the church pastor, many of the people who shared their story before taking the plunge had referenced not so much their relationship with Jesus, but how their life had changed since they connected with the church.

In this not-so-new world, the line still exists. It has simply shifted horizontally.

Sometimes I wonder if all denominationalism has done is rebrand the line. It is still there, just in a slightly different geographical spot. All that has happened is that line-dwelling has moved a little to the left or to the right.

The cut-off of 'What we can get away with?' has simply been redefined from one church network to another. In the same way, the 'How far do we have to go?' has only moved a tad.

Have we been freed from the old law and just replaced it with a new one?

Have we taken off the outdated blindfold only to put on a fresh one?

Has anything fundamentally changed? Or is it just a different set of things to avoid and things to do?

We are like the early explorers who, restricted by fear, would never sail too far in case they fell off the end of the world.

But knights of the Kingdom Principles know there are new lands to discover, new ways to think, new treasures to pursue.

things to learn

No magic wand will instantly change me so I can defeat my foe.

The devil is a title not a name. It means the *accuser* not the *tempter.*

What flows from my heart is the product of what I have first taken in.

I *can* live above the line.

God forms me over time, and I get to partner with Him as He does it.

Worldliness is that which cools my affection towards God.

The Corinthian Church became impotent because of a process . . .

> *Association*
>
> *Attraction*
>
> *Adolescence*
>
> *Arguments*
>
> *Apostasy*

My religion can also lose power because of the same process.

In my world the line may be still there, but it has perhaps only shifted horizontally.

I can use this Kingdom Principle to grow myself over time.

additional notes:

hero

Question: Can you picture courage like this?

A life spent inspiring our children to prove their faith rather than worrying about protecting it, knowing that if their youth is a collection of action and adventure then they will grow to experience His great provision.

A life practicing the presence of God and disciplining ourselves to be quiet enough to recognize His voice, knowing that He will be able speak to us in the noisiest of times when everyone else is panicking.

A life immersed in God's Word rather than simply dipping our toes into it now and again, knowing He will use us to save others.

How stirring would that be?

What could happen if our aim were not simply to be *saved*, but to be *strategic?*

The dragon is terrified of who you are and what you can become.

The rescuer. The hero. The knight in shining armor.

> They overcame him by the blood of the Lamb and by the word of their testimony; they did not love their lives so much as to shrink from death.[106]

Satan not only knows his fate, he knows exactly how it will come about. He will be defeated by an army of saints who overcome their sin and therefore overcome their accuser.

But sin has become confusing. In our desire to explain that all sin separates us from God, and our explanation that it is not just the big sins but the little ones that do this, we have inadvertently inferred something that we should not have.

We have led people to believe that all sin is equal.

This is untrue.

Jesus talks of one person committing a greater sin than his brother, and He teaches that some commandments are more important than others.[107] In our pursuit of the Kingdom, therefore, we are challenged to choose the *greater* good.

I will unpack this in more detail in a future book, but for now we must understand that pursuing the greater good is made possible when we store up good within ourselves.

I thank God for Christianity. We are not force-fed anything; instead we get to choose what we consume.

And we are promised that if we make good investments, we will fulfill our potential.

wilderness

Potential #1: *Store up good, and you can move upwards and onwards.*

How do I tell if I am maturing in my faith? How can I measure my growth? How can I determine my pursuit of holiness? And how does this Kingdom Principle help?

I need to know. I need to find a way to move forward. Fortunately, there *is* a way to do this.

In the life that God promises us, we are not to live on the line, fruitlessly trying to justify our position by comparing ourselves to those around us.

> The Pharisee stood up and prayed about himself: 'God, I thank you that I am not like other men—robbers, evildoers, adulterers—or even like this tax collector.'[108]

God's promise to us is that He does not compare us to His other followers, but to His Son.

Therefore, it is not where we *are* that is important, but which *way we are going*.

If we draw close to Him, He will draw close to us. His promise has little to do with our stationary position, but all to do with the movement of our hearts.

In the television program *Man vs. Wild*, Bear Grylls is parachuted into various remote and dangerous landscapes. No matter what his situation, he gives the same advice to those looking to survive. He advocates that if there is no stream to follow, the best escape is to go in a straight line until you eventually find safety.

What kills you, it seems, is going around in circles. So you stand next to a tree and pick out a marker on the horizon. Once you arrive at the marker, you look back to the tree and follow the line of sight from where you were, past where you are now, to a future point. Once you find a marker on that trajectory, you walk to it and keep on doing this until you get somewhere.

In other words, you have to look back to go forward.

That doesn't sound right, does it?

But if you are moving forward, looking back is actually quite exciting. Looking back shows us how far we have come. Climbing a mountain helps us understand this. As we look forward, the landscape seems to change slowly. But when we look back, we are shocked by the change in landscape. It tells us how far we have come.

According to the Jewish encyclopedia, there are three main categories of sin:

>   *Pesha, Awon,* and *Het.*[109]

These categories give us an opportunity to look back in order to move forward.

>   *Het* is sin we commit when we don't do what we could do.

>   *Awon* is sin we commit when we do what we should not do.

>   *Pesha* is the worst kind of sin where we purposefully break the rules in order to tell God He has no lordship over us.

We've all been there.

We all started in the realm of *pesha*, rebelling against God and crowning our-selves as lord. Many of us have moved on from there. God has already been fulfilling His promise, and we have started to become like Him.

Pesha is the tree we look back at.

Awon is where many of us are now standing.

Het could, in the future, be the only category of sin with which we struggle.

The Kingdom Principle *Rubbish In, Rubbish Out* helps move us away from *pesha*, past *awon*, and beyond *het* as you will see.

We can progress. We can climb that mountain.

pesha

Potential #2: *Store up good, and you can reach your destination.*

Pesha means 'rebellion.' It is derived from *pasha* which means 'to break away from.' It is a willful transgression in order to purposefully depart from the author-ity of the master or from the one who is giving the command.[110]

Jonah was a man who committed *pesha* when, instead of proclaiming God's mes-sage to the city of Nineveh, he purposefully rebelled against God by getting on a ship headed in the opposite direction.[111]

To work out your salvation, you may need to throw your Jonahs overboard.

What Jonah is aboard your boat right now? A habit? An attitude? A person?

Remember, bad company corrupts good character.

Some people will not go on the journey, and some part of us will not either. We are the captain of our own lives, and we can learn from the captain of Jonah's ship.

> The captain went to him and said, "How can you sleep? Get up and call on your god!"[112]

Good advice followed by four questions to ask the Jonahs in our hearts and lives:

> *What kind of work do you do?*
> *Where do you come from?*
> *What is your country?*
> *From what people are you?*

If we store up rebellion, we will eventually act it out.

Surrounding ourselves with rebellious people, attitudes, and habits will allow them to speak too deeply into our lives.

If we do not take action, if we fail to lead ourselves, then our Jonahs can damage us in many ways.

Jonah can become a black hole sucking your time, energy, motivation, and morale.

Jonah brings control. If we do not dictate the course of our lives, our Jonah will.

Jonah brings resentment. When a captain fails to rule a Jonah, he loses respect.

In the Kingdom Principle *Rubbish In, Rubbish Out,* God promises that getting rid of your Jonah will bring about His agenda.

awon

Potential #3: *Store up good, and you can avoid temptation.*

Awon means 'breach.' Derived from a word which means to deviate from something, *awon* is a sin knowingly committed by someone who ultimately wants to do God's will.

It is a sin of commission.

In David's life, the man after God's own heart, he eventually commits a dreadful act. He sleeps with Bathsheba and gets her pregnant. When she informs him of the consequence of his adultery, he first tries to get her husband drunk so that he will sleep with her and think that the baby is his. When this fails, David puts him on the front line of the war and indirectly murders him.[113]

Let me ask you a question, at what point did David get into trouble?

> *In the spring, at the time when kings go off to war, David sent Joab out with the king's men and the whole Israelite army . . . One evening David got up from his bed and walked around on the roof of the palace. From the roof he saw a woman bathing . . . Then David sent messengers to get her. She came to him, and he slept with her . . . The woman conceived and sent word to David, saying, "I am pregnant."* [114]

Was it when God revealed David's sin to a prophet? Was it when Bathsheba became pregnant? No, David was in trouble in the first sentence of the chapter.

> *In the spring, at the time when kings go off to war . . .*

He was not where he should have been.

The devil may be cleverer than us, but it is the small choices that make the difference. Everyone is wise enough to tackle the small temptations. And you can trust the principle to take care of the big ones.

het

Potential #4: *Store up good, and you can raise your expectations.*

Het means 'shortcoming.' It means to miss the mark by not taking an opportunity to do a good deed.

If *awon* is the sin of commission, then *het* is the sin of omission.

So much of the preaching we hear on sin is reactionary instead of proactive.

> If someone hurts you, forgive them.
> If someone takes from you, give him something else.
> If someone abuses you, turn the other cheek.

Perhaps we need to raise our expectations. Perhaps we no longer need to live our lives being worried about being too easily influenced. Perhaps instead, we can harness the fact that we are, and then cultivate the right influences.

We can develop, rather than sear, our conscience.

When I walked away from God at the age of eighteen, I remember feeling horrible when I walked into places I knew I shouldn't. Yet the more often I entered them, the easier it became. I was searing my conscience. My heart muscle was becoming fat as grease. I could not feel it anymore. What I experienced next taught me there is a promise we can hold on to—when we repent, the King can restore to us those sickening feelings that act as trip wires and sound the alarm when we approach danger or danger approaches us.

We can practice the presence of God.

I have a friend who says that he does not pray for an hour in the morning to hear God then, but he prays an hour in the morning so he can hear God while eating pizza at dinnertime. I think this is a halfway mark to a form of cloud-dwelling that Smith Wigglesworth seemed to understand when he said:

> *"I rarely pray for more than thirty minutes. But then thirty minutes rarely goes by without me praying."*

We can take a mental inventory.

> *"Finally brothers, whatever is true, whatever is noble, whatever is right, whatever is pure, whatever is lovely, whatever is admirable—if anything is excellent or praiseworthy—think about such things."*[115]

We can teach in order to learn twice.

It is said that seeing surpasses hearing for information that is retained. And some say that experiencing passes seeing.

This I know for sure . . . the best way to learn something is to teach it!

For some reading this book, the idea of instructing others may seem a step too far.

But that's the point of the principle.

> *"For out of the overflow of the heart, the mouth speaks."*[116]

As good thoughts go in, then good thoughts will naturally come out.

Replace milk with meat, and you can become the teacher.

> *"For though by this time you ought to be teachers, you need someone to teach you again the first principles of the oracles of God; and you have come to need milk and not solid food."*[117]

Replace milk with meat, and you will be surprised what God can do with you!

ambulance

Potential #5: *Store up good, and you can avoid a lot of pain.*

God has two ways of rescuing us.

Fences and *ambulances.*

If you imagine sin as the cliff on the edge of a hill, then the King has put two things in place to rescue you.

There are fences positioned at the top of the cliff. The Jews call these *gezerah*—moral buffers that protect us from going too near the edge. In order to avoid breaking a commandment, the Jews would create a barrier, a religious tradition that would not even allow them to go near the mistake they could potentially make. You can read more about this practice in the first book of the trilogy, *The Line and the Dot.*

Jesus has put fences into our lives: Do not look lustfully at a woman. Do not call someone a fool. Do not hate.

> *"If your eye causes you to sin pluck it out!"*[118]

For Jesus, ignoring these fences was tantamount to falling off the cliff. To Him, everything was a matter of the heart.

In His mind, there is no point biting your tongue; it will only get swollen. If you struggle with your language being crude or vicious or pessimistic, then He tells you to look to your heart. Fill it with the things you wish your tongue to speak.

Then there are the ambulances that wait at the foot of the cliff. They will gather us up when we fall. They will fix us as well as they can, but we may still walk with a limp.

Fences are our friends.

Store them up by seeking, acknowledging, and applying the wisdom of others.

t'shuvah

Potential #6: *Store up good, and return to the joy of how things should be.*

One day I returned home from work to find pink Sharpie markings all over my computer screen and its casing.

I knew it was my son Joel who was four years old then. Whenever I supposed he was the culprit, I would put on my dad's voice, and if Joel cried, I knew he was guilty. So with a calm but deep, booming tone, I called out:

"Joeeel! Come to my office, please."

Two seconds' silence passed and then the whimpering started, followed by the crying, followed by the wailing.

As he walked up the stairs, his Auntie Helen, Auntie Lisa, and Auntie Julie all shouted up to me asking what I was going to do to him. I could tell he had them in the palm of his hands. He was working his crowd with large blue, moist eyes that pleaded, *Don't whip me again, Daddy! Don't whip me!*

By the time he got to the door of my study, he was in that complete state of shock that all four-year-olds go through when they know their end is nigh. Shaking from head to toe, he couldn't get his words out properly and kept repeating, "I'm sorry, I'm sorry!"

I told him that he had been naughty. I told him that it was not just my computer; it was the church's computer. I told him that it would never come off, and to demonstrate that tragedy, I grabbed a piece of cloth and wiped it across the screen.

The pink markings disappeared!

That took me by surprise. What happened next, however, really stunned me. Immediately, as if someone had flicked a switch, Joel changed from a blubbering mess to elation. He threw his hands in the air, beamed like a Cheshire cat and shouted, *"Yippee!"* as he skipped out of my office.

"Come back here, sunshine!" I called, and he returned with his happy face.

"You still did it, you know."
"Yes, Dad, but you wiped it all away."

"Yippees" and skipping continued.

It was the best sermon on redemption I had experienced in thirty years of following Jesus.

Joel was not excited because he would not get smacked as that rarely happened in our house. His real sadness, and therefore elation, came because my ever active child had been stopped from playing downstairs, and now he realized he could get back to the way things should be.

That is what God promises for you and me.

The forgiveness He provides is a way of allowing you to get back to how things should be—your active participation in the joy of God's Kingdom coming to earth.

The Jewish word for repentance is *t'shuvah* which means 'turning and returning.'[119]

Perhaps the biggest failure in the way we repent, that which sometimes stops us from seeing any real change, is our limited understanding of the English word 'repent.'

We *turn*, but we rarely *return*.

We turn away from something and ask forgiveness, but rarely do we pro-actively ask what we should return to.

A great prayer for successful repentance?

> *Turn us to you, O Adonai, and we will be returned.*[120]

T'shuvah can lead you not just to salvation but towards the better you that you can be.

You can be saved, *and* you can be strategic.

ideas to consider

Picture the formation of a new you.

Pioneering something new is a process of four stages (see Book 1 of the Kingdom Trilogy which teaches about Kingdom Pioneers). Each stage requires different skills. Picture the next two stages of your quest, knowing that if you want something to come from your lips, you needed to drink it deeply first. Using this Kingdom Principle to recognize that whatever goes in will eventually come out, create an inventory.

Fill the cloud with the new influences and input you will need to see God move. List the books, sermons, people, and experiences you must store up in your heart to equip you.

KINGDOM PRINCIPLE 4 ⸭ USE IT OR LOSE IT

4

*I vow to be faithful in the little that God has entrusted to me
in order to take hold of the more that He has for me.*

evaluation

Knights fight with what they have been given, not with what they dream of having.

But there is a problem. We must be careful whom we listen to when we evaluate what has been entrusted to us.

For instance, here are a few real life employee evaluations.

> *This young lady has delusions of adequacy.*
> *His men would follow him anywhere . . . but only out of morbid curiosity.*
> *I would not allow this employee to breed.*
> *This employee is depriving a village somewhere of an idiot.*
> *This employee should go far, and the sooner he starts the better.*
> *If you stand close enough to him, you can hear the ocean.*

And my personal favorite:

> *This employee is so dense, light bends around him!*

Many people wish to label us. Some of the descriptions they give us become sticky labels; the longer they remain attached, the harder they are to get rid of. In fact, even after the label is torn off, a residue of glue remains. The sticker has disappeared, but you have to spend what seems like eternity scratching away the goo.

You may change today, but people will not recognize the change until many tomorrows.

God, however, does not place such labels on us.

In fact, He sees the change within us even before we decide to make the transition, and so God's heart is full of hope for you and me.

It has been rightly said that:

> *All souls are precious, but not all are strategic.*

God could not love you more. He does not simply look at the label others have tagged you with, nor does He allow His feelings to be dictated to hy past hurts and failures.

And yet, why is it that so many of us do not live up to what God sees in us?

What obstacles of the mind must be hurdled in order to do so? How do we become tactical to Jesus?

misconception

When Jesus wanted us to understand how strategic we could be to His Kingdom, He made up a story. The complete parable is found in the book of Matthew, but my abridged version is that a master chooses three servants and entrusts them each with a portion of money. To the first he gives five talents; to the second, two; and to the third, one.

The first man invests the five talents and gains five more.

The second invests the two and gains two more.

The third buries his one talent.

Upon his return, the master is pleased with the first two, but declares to the third servant:

> *"You wicked, lazy servant! So you knew that I harvest where I have not sown and gather where I have not scattered seed? Well then, you should have put my money on deposit with the bankers, so that when I returned I would have received it back with interest. Take the talent from him and give it to the one who has the ten talents."* [121]

What makes things worse for those represented by the third servant is that the dragon is a deceiver.

> *He was a murderer from the beginning, not holding to the truth, for there is no truth in him. When he lies, he speaks his native language, for he is a liar and the father of lies.* [122]

He was in the beginning in Genesis when Eve regretted the day *"the serpent deceived me."*[123] He is at the end in Revelation where we hear that *"the devil, who deceived them"* will be thrown into the lake of burning sulfur.[124] The word here for 'deceive' is *planao* which means 'to lead astray.'[125]

The dragon *will* try to deceive you. He will cause you to think you can never be useful to the Lord.

His tactic is to prey on three serious misconceptions, all of which are evident in Jesus' story.

magnet

The first misconception the dragon uses is our understanding of who God is.

The devil preyed upon the third servant's fear of disappointing a fearful master.

> *"I knew you to be a hard man . . . and I was afraid."*[126]

Fear is like a magnet.

Just as faith activates my God, so fear activates my enemy.

It is as though he lies in wait, like a lion on an African plain watching a herd of antelope, searching for the weaker or slower on which to pounce.

> *Be self-controlled and alert. Your enemy the devil prowls around like a roaring lion looking for someone to devour.*[127]

When God provides an opportunity or invites us to participate in some way, our fear may cause us to pass up the request. We say in our minds, "I'll take the next opportunity instead."

The problem is that when the next opportunity comes, our enemy will go back to that same fear. He will push the same button as before.

We must break the cycle before missed opportunity turns to tragic regret.

I wish I didn't have a personal story for this point, but I do.

grandpops

My grandfather was an orphan.

His mother died giving birth to him, and his father died soon afterward from a broken heart. My great grandfather was a local hero who had thrown himself in front of a small train to rescue a colleague and lost a foot in the process. My grandfather was simply a hero to me.

George Gibbs grew up never knowing his parents. Perhaps this is why he had such love for his own family. 'Grandpops,' as he became known to me, was my favorite grandparent. I think it was something about the way he would do any- thing to make me laugh. He looked a little like the professor from *Back to the Future* with his tall, wiry frame and mop of white hair. Making me happy seemed to make him happy.

When I was in my early twenties, Grandpops was diagnosed with cancer. When I heard the news, I immediately got on the train in Manchester to visit him in London. Sitting by his bedside, I could see that this hero of mine, who once could grasp a lamppost and hold himself horizontally in the air, was now a much weaker man. We talked about various things before he finally told me that he knew he was going to die. He wondered if I could tell him how to go to heaven.

It's a funny thing how I can talk to thousands of strangers about my faith with complete courage and conviction, and yet my nerve goes when I wish to broach the subject with a single family member.

What I should have done was simply share the truth of the gospel with him. Instead, I suddenly felt embarrassed by such an intimate question and was reminded of the self-indulgent life I had only recently turned away from. *Who was I to teach anyone?*

I compromised.

I handed him my Bible and pointed out passages that he should read, telling him that he would find the answer in the words of the pages. A few hours later, I caught my train back north.

Within the next few weeks, Grandpops sent me a letter. His hand had obviously lost it firmness, and I struggled to read the scribbled words:

> *Dear Paul,*
> *Thank you for the present. It was one of the nicest things anyone has ever given to me. But I don't understand it. I am still a little afraid. Could you please explain it to me?*

It was like a bullet to my heart. I immediately planned to return to London and do what I should have done in the first place. But before I could go, my mother awoke me early in the morning to tell me that Grandpops had passed away.

The second worst day of my life was the day of his funeral. As I entered the church, my grandmother came to me with tears in her eyes and asked, "Paul, where is he?"

I wanted to say, "Don't worry, Nanny, he is in heaven. And heaven is a wonderful place, let me describe it to you . . . Every tear will be wiped away . . ." But instead, I shrugged. And with much sadness, I uttered the words, "I don't know."

The accuser will accuse you before God. Using every sticky label he can find, he will convince you that you have lost the right to be strategic. He wants you to stagnate, to lie low, to stand still. But you and I have a moral duty; we must share what has been shared with us.

Knights must never be afraid. The results are too fearful to contemplate.

callipers

A second misconception concerns that which God has given us. We can despise our gifts from God when we compare them to what others have received.

What must the third servant have been thinking?

Putting myself in the place of this fictitious character, I imagine him looking down the line as the first of his colleagues receives five talents. Surely he was excited just thinking about what he could achieve with that amount. He then is bemused as the second man receives only two talents. Did he feel sad for him or did he chuckle? Then, with perhaps great embarrassment, he receives just a single talent.

Many of us have experienced this. We looked in the mirror and reflected on the gifts entrusted to others. Our enemy has used that distraction to delude and lead us astray.

Have you ever wondered how valuable the one talent was?

One mina was worth three months' wages, and one talent was equal to sixty minas. Therefore, this single talent represented fifteen years' salary! One mina was worth a lot.

So are you. And so is what the King has invested in you. I know this to be true even though I started with the same misconception.

When I attended North Manchester High School for boys, toughness was evaluated by the number of holes you had in your Doc Martin boots. Sixteen holes was average. Thirty-two holes were only worn by the most elite fighters. I was a small, slender boy and my mother bought me slip-on Doc Martins.

Due to my unfashionable footwear, one of my many nicknames was 'Callipers.'[128] I was never the cool kid, and yet I pioneered an international schools ministry.

> But God chose the foolish things of the world to shame the wise; God chose the weak things of the world to shame the strong.[129]

The writer of those words goes on to declare that God uses the despised things of the world to nullify the things that pretend to be great. No one despises who you are more than the devil.

And those that he despises, he disguises.

He surrounds you with what he portrays as better-looking specimen in order to camouflage your potential, hiding it from your view.

Never despise the day of small things. Small things are much bigger than they first appear to be.

scout

The third misconception involves whose talent it is.

Consider the investment given to the servants. Whose was it?

He entrusted his talents.[130]

It was the master's. It never ceased to be the master's. It was never said that it became the servants'. My problem is that I think what I now have is mine.

But it is not.

It is not for my purpose but His.

When I was in the Boy Scouts, I was very proud to receive two badges. The first was for arts and crafts because I made a papier-mâché crocodile. But my pride and joy was my cooking badge. Did you know that I can go into a farmer's field, create an open fire pit, cook three sausages, and close the pit in such a way that the farmer would never know I had been there?

Impressed? Neither were the girl guides, although it took me awhile to realize it.

For me, those little patches sewn onto my olive green pullover were an opportunity to amaze others and win a date. Surely my papier-mâché crocodile showed my artsy, sensitive side, and my undercover culinary skills declared that at age twelve, I was already a man of mystery!

Silly, of course. But then have any of us really grown up?

My spiritual gifts are not for my benefit or profit. The skills God gave to enhance my life are *for* others.

The supernatural talent that God provides for *their* blessing has been entrusted to *me*.

Three misconceptions, every one a trap set to capture your potential and put it out of circulation.

coin

So, how did David, a teenage boy with all the sticky labels that every adolescent struggles with, go from shepherd boy to the most famous king of all?

His secret lies within his coin.

According to Jewish tradition, when David grew in stature and became king, he commissioned the royal minters to produce a coin that would speak to God's people.

First he commanded that the coin be weighted fairly; this allowed it to become credible beyond the nation of Israel.

Secondly, it was to be stamped on one side with a picture that displayed the majesty of a king God had honored; he chose the imprint to be the tower of David.

The third request, however, took his staff a little by surprise.

> *And on the other side—a shepherd's staff and shepherd's bag.*[131]

The people were thrilled with this decision because the great and mighty David was not ashamed of his humble origin. They said of him:

> *"He never forgets that God had taken him from his flocks of sheep and made him king. He has other flock to care for now, and he treats them as lovingly and as tenderly as he had treated his little lambs!"*[132]

The coin symbolized a characteristic of the God of David's kingdom.

He is looking for those who can be entrusted with a lot because they do not misconceive the power of the little.

He is looking for knights who will use what they have been given.

questions to ask

Who have I listened to when evaluating what has been entrusted to me?

Have I wasted time dreaming of what might be rather than focusing on what is?

I know I am precious to God, but how am I *strategic* to Him?

Which of the three misconceptions do I struggle with most?

>   *A misconception of who God is?*

>   *A misconception of what God has given me?*

>   *A misconception of whose talent it is?*

When I compare my talents to others, how does it make me feel?

Am I using the gifts God has given me or ignoring them while I hunt for others?

If so, what does Jesus' principle teach me will happen?

questions to add:

kerusso

There is one thing Jesus never preached.

He taught about a new kingdom and a new covenant. He described a new kind of worshipper. He unpacked lessons with parables and questions.

But the one thing He never preached?

Beliefs.

Odd, isn't it?

The need for clarity certainly existed in Jesus' day. In fact, far wider doctrinal arguments ensued among those who claimed to be the people of God. One group, for instance, did not believe in the resurrection, angels, or immortality of the soul, and only considered the first five books of the Old Testament authoritative.[133]

And we think we have differences!

So why did Jesus not make doctrinal arguments the key issue?

> Jesus went throughout Galilee, teaching in their synagogues, preaching the good news of the Kingdom . . .[134]

The words for preaching and teaching are different. *Kerusso* is to herald or proclaim. *Didasko* is to unpack the proclamation. What Jesus proclaims is the Kingdom. When He addresses issues of doctrine, it is only in His teaching as He responds to others.

Why?

When God meets man, He does not speak to us about our *beliefs* but about our *behavior.*

Think Ten Commandments.

Think Sermon on the Mount.

Think the Council of Jerusalem.

In a decision taken by those led to govern the new Church, the Gentile converts were told to abstain from food sacrificed to idols.[135] At first this may look like a teaching on beliefs, but the guiding purpose was to allow them to fellowship around the table with their Jewish brothers. It was a decision regarding behavior.

The Greeks worked to shape an individual who would *know* truth.

Jesus worked to shape a community that would *demonstrate* truth.

Modern preaching aims to create *individual* Christians and *educate* them about God's glory.

God's Son aimed to create a *community* that *displayed* God's glory.

Jesus emphasized good news, not simply good education.

The devil has swapped a significant label. We have undervalued behavior and overvalued belief. How can we possibly overvalue belief?

We pay too high a price when we fight over the baubles of our doctrines in such a way that contradicts the Spirit of God.

The Kingdom does not need those who spend their lives in arguments for God; the Kingdom needs those whose life *is* the argument for God.

Beliefs *are* important however. Without believing in Jesus and believing in what He believes in, you can get involved in what the Kingdom of God is doing, but you cannot be a part of it.

But we still face the challenge of the one thing Jesus did not preach.

It prompts the question:

> Do we want to *do* something special or just *believe* something special?

Knights who fight for the heart of the King will not advance God's purposes by simply sieving through doctrines until we have a perfect faith. How can our faith in God be perfect when we cannot yet see God perfectly?

> *For now we see only a reflection as in a mirror; then we shall see face to face. Now I know in part . . .*[136]

And yet our Christian communities seem to prioritize what Jesus did not.

Do you?

Do you want to actively invest in *doing* something special? If so, then we face a second challenge.

What hope do we have of doing something special when we feel that what we have to work with is so small? In fact, how exactly does Jesus equip the weak to confound the wise?

carrots

Knights realize that each quest determines the next.

At the end of Jesus' imaginary tale of the three servants, He leaves us pondering the following Kingdom Principle.[137]

> *For everyone who has will be given more, and he will have an abundance. Whoever does not have, even what he has will be taken from him.* (NIV)

> *For unto every one that hath shall be given, and he shall have abundance: but from him that hath not shall be taken away even that which he hath.* (KJV)

> *To those who use well what they are given, even more will be given, and they will have an abundance. But from those who do nothing, even what little they have will be taken away.* (NLT)

If *Rubbish In, Rubbish Out* is the *formative* principle, then *Use It or Lose It* is the *focal* principle.

It focuses us on what we have and do *now*.

The King wants me to take what He has given me now and invest it wisely, knowing that if I do, He will give me more of the same. If instead I dream about what He might give me, then while I am waiting He will take it away.

God does not use a carrot on a stick.

He does not present us with promises that we will never be able to nibble at. He does not want us to be motivated by what we might get if we serve Him. Instead, He wants us to recognize what we have already been given and realize that we were given it in order to serve others . . . not ourselves.

Line-dwellers are caught calculating a sliding scale between two extremes.

On one end they see effort—on the other, opportunity.

They look for a balance.

They wait for what they *have* to be worth the endeavor.

When it comes to serving God, line-dwellers are enticed by *their* questions:

> *What great thing can you give me to do now?*
> *What great thing can you give me that is worth me doing it great?*
> *What great thing can you give me that will make me be seen as great?*

Cloud-dwellers, however, are encouraged by *His* questions:

> *Will you give Me the little you think you have?*
> *Will you see the greatness in Me that can make your little go a long way?*
> *Will you risk the little you have on those who may have even less?*

Cloud-dwellers do not have a vision of vision. They have a vision of God.

They do not throw away the water they are carrying because they see a mirage.

They do not deal in fantasy. They take hold of reality.

boat

The Kingdom Principle *Use It or Lose It* is not simply a religious statement.

It is life.

It affects everyday living and everyday things. For instance, when Jesus is speaking to the crowds gathered on the shore, He decides to invite a few to follow Him.

> One day as Jesus was standing by the Lake of Gennesaret, with the people crowding around him and listening to the word of God, he saw at the water's edge two boats, left there by the fishermen, who were washing their nets. He got into one of the boats, the one belonging to Simon, and asked him to put out a little from shore. Then he sat down and taught the people from the boat.[138]

What is strange about this story is that He does not choose those sitting eagerly at His feet trying to get His attention. Instead, He turns to Simon and his colleagues as they wash their nets.

Now of course, He needed their boat, but He could have very easily pulled back to shore and gathered disciples from members of the very enthusiastic crowd. Yet He did not.

Jesus got into their boat with an agenda.

If you don't know Jesus has an agenda, then you don't know Jesus.

What He does is interesting to me. He could have chosen disciples from the attentive congregation, but instead chose men who were splitting their attention between His teaching and their work. Perhaps Jesus realized how fickle those sitting in front of Him could be?

Perhaps He knew that the Kingdom requires workers not just dreamers.

Simon would go on to spark a global movement, lead thousands to the Messiah with one sermon, and write a portion of the greatest story ever told.

And yet, it all started with one request:

"Can I use your boat?"

What would have happened if Simon Peter had said no? Would he have delayed the opportunity? Or would he have lost it?

resume

Jesus is summarizing a theme that is seen throughout the Bible.

If I were to ask you to name the top ten famous people in Scripture, I am pretty sure that Elijah and Elisha would pop up on your list. They are of course very much connected. Elisha was the servant of Elijah, a great prophet of the Old Testament.

Elijah's resume is impressive:

Acts of Service
Successfully challenges the priests of Baal on Mount Carmel.[139]
Wipes out many of the prophets of Baal.[140]
Continues to prophesy while persecuted by King Ahab.[141]
Fasts forty days.[142]
Anoints Hazael king over Syria, Jehu king over Israel, and Elisha to be a prophet.[143]

Miracles
Escapes to the wilderness where he is miraculously fed by ravens.[144]
Increases the oil of the widow of Zarephath.[145]
Raises the dead son of the woman of Zarephath.[146]
Causes rain after seven years' drought.[147]
Causes fire to consume the sacrifice.[148]
Calls fire down upon the soldiers of Ahaziah.[149]

Prophecies
Foretells a drought.[150]
Foretells the destruction of Ahab and his house.[151]

Foretells the death of Ahaziah.[152]
Foretells the plague sent as a judgment upon the people in the time of Jehoram.[153]

Red Letter Day
Appears to Jesus at His transfiguration.[154]

Elisha served Elijah well, and God recognized it.

Elisha was no superstar, yet he inherited a double-portion of Elijah's anointing. He was a man who never sought to be in the limelight, but when we study his life, his resume is perhaps even more impressive than Elijah's.

Acts of Service
Instructs that Jehu be anointed king of Israel.[155]

Miracles (not comprehensive)
Divides the Jordan.[156]
Increases the oil of the woman whose sons were to be sold for debt.[157]
Raises the dead son of the Shunammite.[158]
Neutralizes the poison of the pottage.[159]
Increases the bread to feed one hundred men.[160]
Heals Naaman the leper.[161]
Recovers the axe that had fallen into a stream by causing it to float.[162]
Opens the eyes of his servant to see the hosts of the Lord.[163]

Prophecies
Foretells a son to the Shunammite woman.[164]
Foretells death of the unbelieving prince.[165]
Foretells seven years' famine in the land of Canaan.[166]
Foretells death of Benhadad, king of Syria.[167]
Foretells elevation of Hazael to the throne.[168]
Foretells the victory of Jehoash over Syria.[169]

Red Letter Day
Witnesses Elijah's translation, receives a double portion of his spirit.[170]

One prophet passes on to his servant an anointing due to his position. Elijah prophesied, and so did his servant. Elijah performed miracles, and so did his servant. Elijah performed great acts of service, and so did his servant.

Elisha also had a servant. Surely he would follow the same pattern.

Elisha's servant was named _____.

Can you fill in the blank?

Most will not be able to and for good reason.

You would think that Gehazi, Elisha's servant, would carry on the tradition of the prophets. If God were influenced by tradition, position, or sentimentality, you would be right. But He is not.

Take a look at Gehazi's resume:

> Acts of Service
> Nothing of any real note.
>
> Miracles
> None, even though when he was authorized by Elisha, he failed to raise a child from the dead.[171]
>
> Prophecies
> None.
>
> Red Letter Day
> Gehazi is punished with leprosy by Elisha.[172]

Gehazi was faithless with the opportunity given to him. History tells us how he disobeyed his master and fraudulently tried to claim money from Naaman.[173] Perhaps like so many of us, he took it for granted that if he had a position, then the Lord would use him.

In a later story, we get a hint of Gehazi's real issue.

His spiritual immaturity is revealed when, panicking at the sight of an approaching army, he fails to see the supernatural force at his disposal.

> *When the servant of the man of God got up and went out early the next morning, an army with horses and chariots had surrounded the city. "Oh, my lord, what shall we do?" the servant asked. "Don't be afraid," the prophet answered. "Those who are with us are more than those who are with them."*

> *And Elisha prayed, "Open his eyes, Lord, so that he may see." Then the LORD opened the servant's eyes, and he looked and saw the hills full of horses and chariots of fire all around Elisha.*[174]

One of the interpretations of Gehazi's name is 'valley of vision.'[175]

Perhaps that is a good summary of Gehazi's downfall. When we are obsessed with our own vision, we fall into a spiritual valley. Gehazi was primarily interested in his calling, his opportunities, his circumstances. Consequently, he weighed the effort required of him against his potential rewards.

Gehazi's story warns us of the consequences of line-dwelling.

He failed to see God in his vision; therefore, God chose not to see him in His.

things to learn

If we don't know Jesus has an agenda, then we don't know Jesus.

We aim to create individual Christians and *educate* them about God's glory.

God's Son aimed to create a *community* that displays God's glory.

When God meets man, He does not speak to us about beliefs but behavior.

Knights realize that each quest determines the next.

The King wants me to focus on using what He has given me now.

If I use it well, He will give me more.

> *If I use the opportunities He gives me, then more doors will open.*

> *If I waste the opportunities He gives me, the doors may shut.*

> *If I am a good steward of my team, he will bring more experienced people.*

> *If I harvest the wisdom I can from my leaders, He will give me better tutors.*

> *If I neglect Bible reading and prayer, the growth gained will waste away.*

Gehazi's story warns us of the consequences of line-dwelling.

My spiritual gifts are not for my benefit or profit.

The skills God gave to enhance my life are given to others.

additional notes:

possibilities

Question: Can you picture a life like this?

A life where you do not *compete* for fame in a race that others urged you to join, but you *complete* for Him the race that He has set before you, trusting Him to equip you as you go.

A life where you do not rely on luck, changing your mind constantly as you try to guess your next move, but instead you focus on the task in front of you, knowing that God will guide your every step.

A life where you do not flitter away your thinking on foolish disputes, useless contentions, and unprofitable arguments, but faithfully act on what you know is true, certain that the King will prove His existence through your experience.

How purposeful would that be?

The Kingdom of God promises a world of possibilities.

Whereas the global societies of man limit our potential with limitless restrictions—class, race, age, ethnicity, gender, network, and suitability—the Kingdom does not. Most of the heroes of the Bible would never have passed the entrance exam if that were the case.

> *Moses stuttered, David's armor didn't fit, Solomon was too rich, David was too young, Jeremiah was suicidal, Gideon doubted, Samson had long hair, Noah was ridiculed . . . and Lazarus was dead!*[176]

The promise of endless possibilities sets Jesus' dream apart from all other religions. He has a different perspective, an alternative guideline, a specific qualification.

He promises that, in our weakness, we are strong.

In our foolishness, we are strategic.

In our meekness, we are influential.

The *Use It or Lose It* Kingdom Principle reveals an abundance of possibilities when we put it into action. Let me show them to you.

tapestry

Possibility #1: *Use it, and God will weave your story into a masterpiece.*

God does not deal in fate.

At the 2002 World Cup, an interesting poll was taken of English football fans:

> 49% said they would abstain from sex the night before an England game.

> Over 30% said they would be wearing their 'lucky match' boxer shorts.

> 4% said that if their lucky boxer shorts work, they would not wash them until the tournament was over.

But superstitions do not belong in the Kingdom of God.

The Bible does not teach us to trust in luck or fortune. It does, however, mention the *providence* of God. Thirteen times in its pages, the expression means 'to know in advance.' Generally, it denotes God's preserving and governing all things.

Jeremiah 29:11 tells us:

> *"For I know the plans I have for you," declares the Lord, "plans to prosper you and not to harm you, plans to give you a hope and a future."*

The original root word for *plans* is an artistic term that had something to do with weaving. It can also be interpreted as 'meticulous, not left to chance.'

Imagine a tapestry.

On one side the picture is clearly seen, but on the other it is a confusing mish-mash of colors, shapes, and loose threads. Most of these threads represent our choices. Some are good, and some are not so good. The remaining strands symbolize the things that have been done to us. God takes these threads and weaves together the greatest tapestry He can from the choices that we give Him to use. Or, as the writer of Romans put it:

> And we know that in all things God works for the good of those who love him, who have been called according to his purpose.[177]

On our side of the tapestry, we struggle to see the outline, but on God's side, He is weaving the complete story for all to see. *Use It or Lose It* teaches us to entrust to Him the loose threads of our lives.

We are not promised the perfect life but a partnered life.

And our partner is somewhat of a creative genius.

windowsill

Possibility #2: *Use it, and God will breathe new life into you.*

God does not deal in fortunetelling.

The exciting things in life don't come when you aim for them. God brings them into your life when you aim for Him.

The book of Acts records Paul preaching in Troas when a young man, sitting on a windowsill, fell asleep and plummeted out the third story window to his death.

> Paul went down, threw himself on the young man and put his arms around him. "Don't be alarmed," he said. "He's alive!" Then he went upstairs again and broke bread and ate. After talking until daylight, he left. The people took the young man home alive and were greatly comforted.[178]

The sleeper in question is called Eutychus. And his name unfortunately means 'fortunate.'

But it was not fortune that made Eutychus one of the few people in history ever to be raised from the dead. It was something else.

My first thought reading this story is that if anyone fell asleep during one of my sermons, I would certainly jump on his body as Paul did but only to make sure he *stayed* dead!

My second thought is that this story has a great lesson to teach us.

With great courage, Paul rushed out and lay prostrate on the dead body of the young man, Eutychus. Paul was brave, not simply for attempting to raise Eutychus from the dead, but also for how he did so. He associated himself with both Elijah and Elisha who did similar things in a similar way.[179] He wanted to make sure his audience knew he represented the same God.

It was Saturday night.

The Jews had enjoyed the Sabbath, and when it finished (when the first three stars are seen in the sky), the Gentiles joined them for teaching and fellowship. It is likely, therefore, that Eutychus joined the Jews after *their* Sabbath, but not *his*.[180]

He had been working hard at a manual job all day.

There are no FYIs in the Bible. No throwaway trivia. The mention of many lighted lamps is there for a reason. Many lamps indicated four things:

Lots of heat.

Lots of smoke.

Lots of stuffiness.

And little oxygen.

Eutychus was sitting on the windowsill in order to get a little fresh air and stay awake. He used the little time and energy he had to put himself before God, and God granted him an entire second life.

There was something attractive to God about Eutychus.

Eutychus was on the windowsill of God's mind.

consecration

Possibility #3: *Use it, and it will accumulate interest.*

Not fortune, flashiness, or favoritism, but *faithfulness* puts us on the windowsill of God's mind.

> *Without faith it is impossible to please God . . .*[181]

Faithfulness is consecration in overalls.

When we come to God, we are set apart *by* Him, and we are to set apart our lives *for* Him.

But how does consecration work?

It is like promising God five dollars. We hand over the note, and He passes it right back to us, requesting that we take it to the bank and exchange it for five hundred pennies. Every so often He will ask us for one of those pennies that we already promised Him.

Every penny represents a choice. An action. A *doing* of something.

Salvation comes when we consecrate ourselves to God. But consecration is not a one-off commitment. It consists of daily one-cent decisions that we make for His Kingdom.

As my mum used to say, "If you look after the pennies, the pounds will take care of themselves."

Spiritual growth can occur both *incidentally* and *intentionally.* But the results of each are vastly different.

For instance, two people may receive a free one year apprenticeship with the Pais Project. One will grow a little simply because of the environment, teaching, and opportunity. Another will grow far more by being intentional. They actively study the notes they take; they try as hard as they can when empowered; they ask lots of questions of their leaders. The same opportunity is given, but two different levels of growth are achieved.

Knights are intentional. They are faithful with the pennies God gives them.

As you desire rather than despise the day of little things, then be assured that those small gifts that you hand back to your King will gain interest. Your pennies will turn into pounds.

doris catherine gibbs

Possibility #4: *Use it, and God will move heaven and earth.*

When I was about to transition into high school, my parents were given options of where to place me. The high school they wanted to choose, however, was not listed. When they inquired about it, they were told that particular school had no vacancy and a very long waiting list.

My mother refused to send me to any of the alternatives, and after weeks of wrangling, she kept me home from school for the first few days of my higher education. Eventually, my parents were threatened with legal action and sent a wider list of alternative schools.

My mum was stubborn.

And clever. She chose the one school on the list that she knew would never accept me.

King David High. An all-Jewish school.

The campus was less than one hundred yards from our house, and there were no legal reasons preventing me from going. Only religious ones. The headmaster of the school showed up twice over the following days to desperately plead with my parents not to send me to his school. According to my father, on his second visit, he practically shed a tear and, after leaving, pleaded with the Education Department not to send me to his school.

Soon afterwards, my mother's first choice school mysteriously opened up.

My mother loved me and wanted me to be taught in the best possible place. She moved heaven and earth for me to go to the school which, at the time of my acceptance, had the best local reputation.

It was at this school that I met the teacher responsible for leading me to Christ. God could rely on Simon Newbury to share his faith with me. As a teacher, he may have not been the coolest or the most popular, but he was, without doubt, faithful to his God. The Father knew that if He could just get me to Mr. Newbury, Mr. Newbury would take care of the rest.

And so, here is my question: Would God move heaven and earth so that those He loves can come into contact with you?

The promise of God is that, if you are faithful, He will do just that!

tortoise

Possibility #5: *Use it, and you will win the good race.*

I am the tortoise not the hare.

Are you familiar with Aesop's fable?

In the tale, a hare ridicules a slow-moving tortoise, so the two race to determine who is faster. The hare soon leaves the tortoise behind and, confident of winning, decides to take a nap midway through the course. When he awakes, however, he finds that his competitor, crawling slowly but steadily, has reached the finished line first.

That has been my experience. Some people start off with more ability, charisma, and qualification than others. Yet not all of them consistently grow. Some may, but some may not.

It is not what you have been given but what you *do* with it that is significant.

No matter how few teams Pais had or how little the financial resources were, I have learned not to despise what God has entrusted to me when comparing it to others. Some of my friends have even told me they are a little surprised with where Pais is now.

I was once told that Pais had a 'poverty mentality.' I don't think we do. I think we have a 'stewardship mentality.' We will never likely have much money in the bank, because our vision and capacity has increased with our funding. But in the day of small things, we learned how to make virtually no money go a long way. Now we are making a lot more money go a lot further than perhaps many others would know how to.

Necessity is the mother of invention.

I wish I were fast, but I am not. I am slow but steady.

I am steady like the hill walker who plods up the hill at what feels like a slow pace, but every time he looks around, he is surprised to see how much the scenery behind him has changed.

The scenery does change, doesn't it?

The reality is that only space cadets look out of a window at the same thing day after day. We are in an ever-changing world.

So, as the world at large changes, so does our journey. If you are faithful, then don't be surprised when new and possibly scary opportunities open up for you. Don't worry that you do not feel ready; you are probably much more ready than you think.

Remember, prophecies don't shape us; principles do. And if you've been shaped by this principle, you will be ready for anything.

We don't live by fate.

We live by faith.

ideas to consider

Picture a tapestry, and focus on the side God sees.

Imagine the greatest story God can weave. See yourself handing Him beautiful threads that are both long and strong to work with as well as the loose ones that you don't know how He can use. Envision yourself faithfully acknowledging all that God has entrusted to you and investing it wisely.

Fill in the cloud with opportunities that God is currently giving you.

KINGDOM PRINCIPLE 5 ✦ REAPING AND SOWING

*I vow to sow seeds into my life that will produce fruit
for the Kingdom of God.*

arrows

Knights fight battles in distant lands.

If I were to pick one passage of scripture to describe the work of Pais, it would be Psalm 127. The first part goes like this:

> *Unless the LORD builds the house, the builders labor in vain. Unless the LORD watches over the city the guards stand watch in vain. In vain you rise early and stay up late, toiling for food to eat—for he grants sleep to those he loves.*

I understand that Pais is a work that God has to build—I cannot. The fact that God is involved leads me to another important conclusion: We cannot build any-thing worthwhile in a moment.

The poem continues:

> *Children are a heritage from the LORD, offspring a reward from him. Like arrows in the hands of a warrior are children born in one's youth. Blessed is the man whose quiver is full of them. They will not be put to shame when they contend with their opponents in court.*[182]

The spiritual fight that God has called us into does not simply involve hand-to-hand battle. He is imploring us to shape the future.

As a missionary who makes missionaries, I see the young people we disciple like arrows that we are preparing and shooting into a fight where we cannot go. We fire them into the offices, the factories, the courthouses, and the universities where we will never tread.

It is a battle of faith where we believe what we do *now* will make a difference *then.*

But this kind of battle can drain us.

And herein lies the problem.

Expending effort with no guarantees of when things will pay off is not what many of us are accustomed to doing. We want to know *when our efforts will be reward-ed and how.*

Why should I have to invest so much now, not knowing where it might lead?

Would it not be better if God set deadlines and pay dates?

scorpion

Jesus paints a wonderful picture filled with hope, but only hints at what is to come. He is not explicit about times and dates. Instead He urges us to build towards something very cool, somewhere under wraps, at some time in the future.

Why would the Father tease us?

> *No one knows about that day or hour, not even the angels in heaven, nor the Son, but only the Father. As it was in the days of Noah, so it will be at the coming of the Son of Man.*
>
> *Therefore keep watch, because you do not know on what day your Lord will come. But understand this: If the owner of the house had known at what time of night the thief was coming, he would have kept watch and would not have let his house be broken into. So you also must be ready, because the Son of Man will come at an hour when you do not expect him.*[183]

He seems to be stressing the importance of being prepared for His coming, while purposely withholding any real clue as to when that might be.

Why?

First of all, we have to understand that Jesus agreed with His fellow sages about the Judgment Day. Much of what He says about His coming seems to be in line with their thinking. His statements seem to be more like reminders than something totally new.

What makes Jesus' statement different from His contemporaries is that they believed that the coming of the Messiah and the Day of Judgment would be simultaneous. Jesus, however, teaches His disciples that these two events will not happen together. He, the Messiah, has come; yet there is still time to get ready. So how much time do we have?

We do not know. And there is a reason for that.

There is a reason why this is hidden, why it is not yet being disclosed, and why you and I should not waste time trying to work it out.

It was said by these sages:

> "May the bones of those who calculate the end be blasted away." [184]

Why would the rabbis so harshly warn people not to spend their time calculating the end? You may find the answer quite shocking.

Because they also said:

> "It has been taught that three things come when the mind is diverted: the Messiah, finding a lost article, and a scorpion. So don't postpone His coming by thinking about it!" [185]

I was taught as a young man that we can speed up the coming of Christ by reaching the whole world with His message. Now here, the writing of Jesus' colleagues suggest that we can also slow it down.

Can this be true? If so, why?

On a road trip back from California, my family and I pulled in to a New Mexico motel. It had the usual simple set up—just two double beds and a shower. I was dead tired and hoped for a sound sleep before completing the second leg of our journey.

Unfortunately, a small circumstance prevented that.

A scorpion.

It was the first time I'd seen a scorpion in real life, and I certainly wasn't expecting to see one ambling along the side of my bed. I was quite sleepy, but I still panicked. My tired mind went through a questioning process:

> *There's a scorpion in my bedroom! Is this usual? Is it dangerous?*
> *Should I just leave it? Should I get rid of it? How do I get rid of it?*

For a moment I considered letting it go, hoping it would crawl back outside. I am one of those people who doesn't find it easy to kill insects. Instead, I spend considerable time hunting them down, catching them in paper cups to re-enact the *Born Free* film, and setting them loose in my garden. The idea of hurting this scorpion that seemed so little was troublesome to me. It was only small and fairly transparent.

Could it really do that much damage?

But then I imagined one of my sons going to the bathroom in the middle of the night and stepping barefoot on it. I decided not to take the risk and squashed it with my shoe. Only later did I find out that with this particular scorpion, it was exactly the right thing to do![186]

My biggest problem with the scorpion was that I was not expecting it and was therefore unable to handle it.

If we expect things, we tend to *handle* them. Our humanity wants to *handle* God. We secretly hope to force Him into some kind of deal. Deadlines and deals seem to go hand in hand.

But God is not only *unimaginable*. He is also *unmanageable*.

virgins

Could it be that God purposely wants us to be ready but not expectant?

Why? Because our readiness will be more genuine.

If we are expecting God to turn up and judge us, we are more likely to be doing the things He tells us to only to avoid punishment or gain a reward. If we are not expecting it, then our actions are more likely to be motivated by authentic faith and a genuine love for the things He loves.

Many of us are tempted to give depending upon what we will get in return. Rather than becoming bold knights, we waste energy calculating the risks.

Jesus warns against this with His story of the ten virgins. These young women took their lamps and went out to meet the bridegroom. Five foolishly took their lamps but no extra oil, while five wisely took oil in jars along with their lamps. As they waited for the bridegroom to arrive, the five foolish virgins ran out of oil and had to go buy more. But while they were on their way to buy some, the bridegroom arrived. The virgins who were ready went in with him to the wedding banquet, and the door was shut. When the five foolish virgins returned, they were turned away.[187]

The story of the ten virgins speaks to us of purity.

Not a purity of body, but a purity of heart.

Not simply a purity of heart, but specifically a purity of *motive*.

The oil in the lamps would have lasted for fifteen minutes, usually enough time to respond to the sudden arrival of the groom. Five of the young ladies had calculated exactly how much oil they needed to purchase and put in their lamps so as not to waste any. The wise virgins, however, had filled their lamps and spent more than they thought they probably needed to ensure they would be ready when their moment came.

The error of the foolish virgins was not that they were cheap. No, they rushed out to spend more money on oil. Their mistake was that they tried to work out in advance precisely how much oil they needed to fulfill their duty.

And here's the rub. Could it be that, for many of us, our morality has become a question of working out just how much we must do to meet the deadline?

God does not have *favorites*.

But He does show *favor.*

Could it be He is looking to show favor to a different kind of person who practices a different kind of morality? Does the King really want us to consciously think, *Could it be today? Could it be tomorrow?*

Or is He looking for those aware that He will return, but focused less on what will happen to *them then* and more on what happens to *us now*?

As Jesus continued to speak in parables, He implied an important question:

Who will be the *good* servants?

The good servants are those He describes whose service is not swayed by how much time it takes for the master to return, but by how much of themselves they have invested now.[188]

The Father is calling you not to a *deadline*, but to become a *lifeline*.

Knights, as I have said, go on a quest.

Medieval knights pursued treasure, and their quest was rewarded by their King. The knights of the Kingdom Principle are also rewarded with treasure, but in this upside-down Kingdom, they do not pursue it.

They instead pursue His heart.

questions to ask

Deep down do I want to manage God?

Do I broker deals with Him?

If I do, in what areas of my life do I do this?

Which group of virgins would I most likely have been in and why?

> *The wise group?*

> *The foolish group?*

Do I calculate the risks? If so, how does this affect my faith?

Why would God ask me to invest so much now yet not guarantee where it will lead?

Why would it be wrong for God to set deadlines and pay dates?

What would 'ready but not expectant' look like in my life?

How pure are my motives?

questions to add:

REAPING AND SOWING || THE PRINCIPLE

subliminal

Knights of the Kingdom are trained.

According to a study by the United States National Research Council, Americans spent fifty million dollars in a single year on subliminal message tapes. They played these soundtracks while they slept or as a background noise while concentrating on other things. The hope was that these tapes would help them in several areas of their conscious lives—for instance, to improve their self-image or stop smoking cigarettes. The NRC's verdict, however, contained no subconscious message. They stated the results simply: "They don't work."

The tapes failed to produce the power needed.

Jesus' advice is in no way subliminal:

> For out of the overflow of the heart the mouth speaks. The good man brings good things out of the good stored up in him, and the evil man brings evil things out of the evil stored up in him.[189]

On several occasions, Jesus emphasized various aspects of this Kingdom Principle which was already understood by the ancient knights of God.[190]

To remind us of His words, the writer of Galatians succinctly states it this way:[191]

> Do not be deceived: God cannot be mocked. A man reaps what he sows. (NIV)

> Be not deceived; God is not mocked: For whatsoever a man soweth, that shall he also reap. (KJV)

> Don't be misled—you cannot mock the justice of God. You will always harvest what you plant. (NLT)

If *Use It or Lose It* is the *focal* principle, then *Reaping and Sowing* is the *futuristic* principle. We sow into the future with no strings attached.

This principle advises us to work towards that which will promote the success of the Kingdom. The consequence is that God will ensure that whatever we sow now, we will all reap later.

God is giving us shares in the future. How often do we hear that?

In our world of instant, we are not used to this truth. In fact, we pay for things *after* we have already received them. The world has seen for itself the disastrous results of a culture of credit. The labels of our provision have been swapped.

Where God intended to give us stock now in something that will pay off later, the enemy entices us with the self-gratification of receiving now and paying later.

We then stare at the line, wondering when our reward will come to us. The less faith we have in this Kingdom Principle, the more we edge toward its extremes. And the further away our reward seems, the less risks we take.

When it comes to investing in the future, line-dwellers are goaded by *their* questions:

> *What is the timeline?*
> *Is there a shortcut?*
> *What can I do now that will benefit me soon?*

Cloud-dwellers, however, are guided by *His* questions:

> *Will you commit to My process?*
> *Will you trust in My strategy?*
> *What will you do now so that others can benefit from it in the future?*

The sowing by cloud-dwellers is not artificially increased the more it smells sulfur or hears a harp.

Cloud-dwellers are not accessing spiritual health insurance.

This is not bargain seed.

This is the spiritual mechanism by which we help shape the future.

surf

We must stop *trying*.

And start *training*.

When I first decided to go surfing, I prepared all year. By preparation I mean I grew my hair, learned the lingo, and bought board shorts. I rented a surfboard and hit the beach, then paddled out and waited.

Suddenly, I was in the perfect place to catch the perfect wave. One guy even shouted across to me, *"This one's got your name on it!"*

I tried to catch the gnarly monster but failed completely. The waves on Fistral Beach, Cornwall, tossed me around like a rag doll, and I eventually flopped back onto the sand.

I had *tried*, but I had not *trained*.

Line-dwellers look for instant success, and when they see an opportunity, they give it their best shot.

Cloud-dwellers sow. They train, and when their opportunity arrives, they catch it.

Faith is not in the stepping out. Faith is in the waiting.

delayed

The Kingdom Principle *Reaping and Sowing* encourages us to sow into the future by investing in our present.

Life has a delayed reaction.

After stopping for drinks at an illegal bar, a Zimbabwean bus driver found that the twenty mental patients he was supposed to be transporting from Harare to Bulawayo had escaped. As you might expect, he panicked.

However, you probably wouldn't guess what he did next.

Not wanting to admit his incompetence, the driver went to a nearby bus stop and offered everyone in the line a free ride. He then delivered the passengers to the mental hospital, telling the staff that the patients were very excitable and prone to bizarre fantasies.

The deception wasn't discovered for three days.

It would be much simpler, I think, if the moment you sinned there was an instant consequence.

The businessman's gospel might then be this: *Sin today, and the profits fall; recommit tomorrow, and clients roll through the door.*

A parent's faith could look like this: *Pray one week, and your children become little angels, minding their 'P's and 'Q's and never embarrassing you in public again; sin the next week, and they transform into the spawn of Satan.*

The pastor's ministry could demonstrate this: *Sin one week, and the congregation attendance drops; repent the following week, and revival occurs.*

Why does God seem to have gotten this so wrong?

Maybe I should correct Him.

After all, if instant consequences were the norm, then perhaps the whole world would recognize the Word of God to be authentic. All people would follow Him, because they would not dare do otherwise.

God's dream, however, does not work that way, and I believe there is an important reason for this.

God wants friendship.

He wants us to serve Him because we love Him. He wants us to obey Him because we believe Him. He wants us to become like Him because we can.

artificial

I once read about a Russian leader who, as a child, attended Sunday school. The class was fairly disruptive, so the priest in the village of Kalonovka decided to reward any good behavior with candy. Our young friend responded especially well to this treatment and recited the Scriptures with great gusto and piety. The priest noticed this young man and took him under his wing, using various treats and rewards to induce great results from him. The young boy won prizes for memorizing and reciting scripture.

This young man grew up to become the first Communist Czar, Nikita Khrushchev, who eventually declared that God did not exist.

Artificial rewards produce artificial results.

In my desire to raise up a generation to help redeem their world, I understand the need for leaders who can pass on real faith. We must not water down the calling or make it about rewards, either now or in the future.

We want to go beyond *presentation* to *provocation*.

We don't want to entertain. We want to disciple. That requires not an attractive light show, but an attractive discipler.

We serve an authentic God who loves authentic people and wants them to live an authentic life.

We are to be about the Kingdom not karma.

karma

In a BBC poll, Winston Churchill was voted the greatest Briton who ever lived.[192] His philosophy on relationships was as follows:

> *"I have no secret. You haven't learnt life's lesson well if you haven't noticed that you can give the tone or color, or decide the reaction you want of people in advance. It's unbelievably simple. If you want them to smile then smile first. If you want them to take an interest in you then take an*

interest in them first. If you want to make them nervous then become nervous yourself. If you want them to shout and raise your their voices, then raise yours and shout. If you want them to strike you, strike first. It is as simple as that. People will treat you like you treat them. It's no secret. Look about you. You can prove it with the next person you meet."

Churchill loved an empire. Jesus loves a Kingdom. And there is a difference.

The empire builder says, "Do unto others, *and* they will do to you."

The Kingdom builder says, "Do unto others *as* you would have them do unto you." [193]

No promises of instant reciprocation. No strings attached. We sow not for our instant comfort, but to create future culture.

Churchill was preaching karma.

Karma is the belief that what we do now entirely shapes our future. What goes around, comes around. The circle of life. Christians can become *karma chameleons* in that we transfer the values of karma onto the teaching of Jesus.

Yet, the teaching of Jesus differs in at least two important ways:

Grace and *Kingdom*

Love interrupts. It puts a grace-shaped kink in the wheel.

Love for us means that God is not bound by some universal law. His mercy can kick in at any moment, unplanned but never unwanted.

His love for others means that the Kingdom Principle *Reaping and Sowing* is not for our benefit, but for the benefit of the Kingdom.

Karma promotes self-preservation; the Kingdom promotes faithful service.

culture

The promise that 'what we reap we will sow' allows us to shape our culture, whether that be the culture of our family, church, community, organization, or whatever.

If we sow gossip, we will reap mistrust.

If we sow disrespect, we will reap rebellion.

If we sow apathy, we will reap failure.

If we sow love, however, we will reap the kind of love we sow.

If you speak when you are angry, you will deliver the best speech you will ever regret.

The longer we lead, the more we see those we lead become a mirror image of ourselves. This Kingdom Principle, therefore, encourages me to use it to create the culture I want to see. I do not have to be a fashion icon, charismatic, or the world's greatest preacher to shape the future of the organization God has called me to lead.

I just have to *be* what I want to *see*.

The principle will ultimately affect our worship of God.

I heard a tale once about a kingdom that was suffering a terrible drought. The king asked his people to bring all the water they had for the sake of the nation. He forced no one, but instead requested that they bring as much water as they could spare. Some brought a barrel full. Some brought a thimble full. Some brought a cart full. Some brought a cup full. When they arrived at the castle, the king thanked them and, taking their water, poured it into his moat so that the rich and the poor could come to the castle for water when they were in need.

As a thank you to his people, he invited them into the palace and showed them his treasury. The gigantic room was filled with precious metal and jewels. There were golden shields and emerald necklaces, silver spears and diamond rings.

The king turned to the people and said, "You can each take whatever you like as long as it fits into the container in which you brought your water."

So it is with our worship of God. Whatever we bring into His throne room often determines how much we leave with.

Our heart is the container. Our attitude determines its size.

power

Let me share a poem to help us see the opportunity that God provides:

> *Sow a thought, reap a word;*
> *sow a word, reap a deed;*
> *sow a deed, reap a habit;*
> *sow a habit, reap a character;*
> *sow a character, reap a destiny.*[194]

The Father is providing us with real power.

The power to partner with Him.

The power to shape the destiny of many.

things to learn

God does not have favorites, but He does show favor.

God cannot be deceived.

He will ensure that whatever we sow now, we will all reap later.

He is giving us shares in the future.

I must stop *trying* and start *training*.

Faith is not in the stepping out. Faith is in the waiting.

Life has a delayed reaction.

Artificial rewards produce artificial results.

We are to be about the Kingdom not karma.

> *Karma excludes grace. Reaping includes love.*

> *Karma is self-absorbed. Kingdom is selfless service.*

We can shape the culture of our lives, family, church, neighborhood, etc.

We do this by being what we want to see.

Our heart is the container. Our attitude determines its size.

additional notes:

KINGDOM PRINCIPLE 5

REAPING AND SOWING ||THE PROMISE

sowing

Question: Can you sow into a life like this?

A life not wasted by wishing you could change the past, but instead concentrated on the here and now, knowing the King will multiply the investments you make into the future.

A life where you do not jump ship hoping for a better journey, but instead stay the course you have been given by God, knowing that if you make good turns, you will reap a more exciting journey.

A life where, rather than holding onto your loved ones, you give them away, confident that they will return bigger, better, and bolder than when they left.

How rewarding would that be?

Medieval knights pursued treasure, and their king rewarded them. Likewise, the knights of the Kingdom Principles are rewarded, but in this upside-down Kingdom, they don't pursue the reward.

They simply sow good seed.

God promises that good seed will reap a good harvest.

However, others may reap that harvest.

> *Whatever a man sows . . .*

We have individualized the principle, oblivious of the fact that the word 'man' can also mean 'humankind.'

Cloud-dwellers live with the understanding that the seed they sow is not only affecting their own future, but also the destiny of others.

God does not simply deal with us as individuals; He deals with us as communities. Joshua sowed a good report but still reaped forty years in the wilderness.[195]

It is a test of motives.

You may sow, but others may reap.

And the promise is that what we do today will not only be reaped by us, but also by those we know and don't know.

What an opportunity!

Jesus' principle promises many opportunities. Let me show you a few.

billy

Opportunity #1: *Sow, and you will reap the same kind as you sow.*

> *"Likewise, every good tree bears good fruit, but a bad tree bears bad fruit. A good tree cannot bear bad fruit, and a bad tree cannot bear good fruit."*[196]

Billy Graham, the internationally famous evangelist, once came to Britain and powerfully shared the message of Jesus in a way relevant to that time. Twelve years later he returned, and as was the custom, he preached while fifty-two ministers sat on the stage behind him. Every one of the fifty-two ministers had reportedly become followers of Jesus as a result of his previous visit.

Billy reaped the same kind as he had sown.

neighbor

Opportunity #2: *Sow, and you will reap in a different season than when you sow.*

When my bride and I moved into our first home, I hoped to share my faith with my next-door neighbor, yet for many months, I struggled to create an authentic opportunity. One day, as I was putting my suitcase in my car about to set off for a leadership conference, my neighbor popped out and asked to speak with me. I was already running late and told him that I would love to chat the following week as soon as I returned. He smiled politely and said that would be fine.

But something inside me said that it wouldn't be fine at all.

So I changed my mind and followed him inside the house. In a typically English way, we spent the first fifteen minutes sipping cups of tea and talking about the weather until finally he shared his problem. He asked me if I had known that his wife had once been a prostitute. I replied that I did not. And so, he went on to share the sad story of their rocky marriage, ending with the following summary and question:

> *"Paul, today I spoke to her sister who told me that she has been sleeping with two of my friends. She left me last week and has run out of money. And her family has just informed me that she has been going out to night clubs and paying the taxi drivers with sexual favors . . . I know you are a Christian. What should I do?"*

I had no idea! I had never dealt with a situation like this. What I wanted to do was hand him my pastor's business card in a similar way that I handed my grandfather my Bible. But I had learned my lesson. Instead, I asked him a few questions, more out of the need to create space to think than out of curiosity. I used those few moments to practice what I had been learning for months on Tuesday nights at my church—to hear God's voice.

Some thoughts that seemed wise—too wise to be my own—popped into my mind. I shared them with him, and he said they really helped. I was in my early twenties trying to advise a man twice my age. But the months sown into me as I committed to the Tuesday night Bible study at Sharon Church had prepared me for this moment.

I did not have to *try*. I had been *trained*.

What was sown in one season had paid off in another.

winter

Opportunity #3: *Sow, and you will reap in proportion to what you sowed.*

> *"Give, and it will be given to you. A good measure, pressed down, shaken together and running over, will be poured into your lap. For with the measure you use, it will be measured to you."* [197]

The more we sow, the more we reap.

And so, let me share this advice with you. *Never cut down a fruit tree in winter.*

We may have the courage to take that first step of faith, but faith is in the waiting, and while we are waiting, winter can come and go. In winter, things look bleak. The tree looks bare, perhaps even dead. But what we cannot see is the growth beneath the ground. The tree is still alive. It's still healthy. It's preparing to produce fruit.

Don't downsize your vision in times of trouble.

Keep on sowing as you first believed you should. Do not recalculate your sacrifice or rescale the dream that God gave you.

You will reap in proportion to *what* you sowed, not what you *hoped* to sow.

time

Opportunity #4: *Sowing today affects the future, not the past.*

Around twenty years ago, a lady in my church told me God was calling me to Zaire.

It was a bit of a shock.

I politely explained that I felt she was mistaken but thanked her for her prayers. She was a wonderful lady, and because I respected her so much, I struggled for a while with the conversation. She was no fruitcake but instead much admired by everyone. Years later, all was revealed by one of her family members.

It seems that when she was a young lady, she felt called to serve the people of Zaire. After raising support, she began to make plans. Also around that time, she fell in love with a young man and they got engaged. At first, it seemed to be the perfect love story until she realized he had no intention of being a missionary in Africa. She had a choice, and she chose him. Eventually, the engagement fell apart, and for some reason, it had become too difficult for her to leave England.

As the person telling me the story finished, his summary of her life was etched into my mind:

> *Since then, whenever she has seen somebody with a bit of spark, she has told them that they are called to Zaire. You were not the first person, and probably not the last. It is as though she's trying to fill the place in Africa that she felt God had called her to fill.*

What a sad story.

The two saddest words in the English dictionary are *'if only.'*

A survey of retired Americans proves that. One of the top four regrets in life was:

> *Not taking more risks.*[198]

We all live with regret. Yet Jesus encouraged us not to worry about the past but instead invest our time into the future. He prompts us to hold onto another of the Father's pledges:

> *". . . I will restore to you the years that the locust hath eaten . . ."*[199]

If we repent of our mistakes and invest our time in sowing into the future, He will return us to how things can be and will do it more quickly than we would expect.

wesley

Opportunity #5: *We will reap when we stay around until harvest time.*

> *Those who sow in tears will reap with songs of joy. He who goes out weeping, carrying seed to sow, will return with songs of joy, carrying sheaves with him.*[200]

John Wesley reportedly awoke each morning at five o'clock for prayer and Bible study. Eight thousand miles on horseback was his annual record as he traveled from place to place sharing his faith. He wrote more than forty books, some of which were penned while riding his horse, and they were so cheap even the poor could buy them.

He founded dispensaries for the sick, homes for orphans, schools for the working class, and he opposed slavery.

None of this happened in a moment. He lived to be 87 years old, and I believe this summarization of his journal hints at the secret of his victorious life.

> Sunday, A.M., May 5
> Preached in St. Anne's. Was asked not to come back anymore.
>
> Sunday, P.M., May 5
> Preached in St. John's. Deacons said, "Get out and stay out."
>
> Sunday, A.M., May 12
> Preached in St. Jude's. Can't go back there either.
>
> Sunday, A.M., May 19
> Preached in St. Somebody Else's. Deacons called special meeting and said I couldn't return.
>
> Sunday, P.M., May 19
> Preached on street. Kicked off street.
>
> Sunday, A.M., May 26
> Preached in meadow. Chased out of meadow, as bull was turned loose during service.
>
> Sunday, A.M., June 2
> Preached out at the edge of town. Kicked off the highway.
>
> Sunday, P.M., June 2
> Afternoon, preached in a pasture. Ten thousand people came out to hear me.[201]

Many would have given up by May 19th.

Many sow but do not reap.

Countless times I have seen young leaders deceived by the culture of instant rewards. They give in to poor advice which tells them that their winter should not be a time of discontent, and that discontent can never be God.

This promise, however, says stick around, stick at it, because harvest time *will* come.

gym

Opportunity #6: *Sow, and the Spirit increases your energy to sow more.*

Scripture unpacks the Kingdom Principle further by saying:

> *"Let us not become weary in doing good, for at the proper time we will reap a harvest if we do not give up."*[202]

After more than two decades of battle, I have come to understand that this is easier said than done.

Many years ago, I joined a gym. The facility was technologically advanced, and I was told that before I joined they would need to run a physical analysis of my body. They hooked me up to various machines and ran tests which my fitness instructor explained would be summarized on a sheet of paper. After twenty minutes of hell, the young sadist wafted in front of me, not so much a sheet of paper but more like a scroll. This declaration of decrepitness went from shoulder height to the floor. She then asked me what my physical targets at the gym might be.

Looking at the analysis, I thought to myself, "Well, staying alive might be nice!"

After explaining that some people come to lose weight, some to prepare for a marathon, and some to regain shape after giving birth, she advised that I work on my low blood pressure.

I struggled with her proposal. I was preparing to go to the gym with a friend of mine who is much taller and broader than I am. When we exercised in front of the mirror, he looked like a beefcake while I resembled a cupcake! I needed more of a manly motive than working on my blood pressure, and so I asked her to defend her suggestion.

She then described in uncanny detail how I would come home from working in retail and be lethargic, depleted of all energy, and crash onto the sofa for the night.

"Mr. Gibbs, you will have no energy unless you expend some."

So true.

arthur

Opportunity #7: *We sow seed, and God adds a supernatural blessing.*

What we give may seem very small, but if it is the best we can do, magic happens.

Arthur Stace was an illiterate, homeless alcoholic living on the streets of Sydney, Australia. A veteran of the Great War, he returned home from France partially blind in one eye and suffering the effects of poison gas. During the Great Depression, he deteriorated further until he was drinking methylated spirits at six pence a bottle.

On August 6, 1930, he went as he had done many times before to Saint Barnabas' Church. He prepared to sit through the obligatory sermon before he could receive the free food. However, on this day, he slipped to his knees and prayed for the first time. A few months later at another church, he heard the preacher shout:

"I wish I could shout eternity through all the streets of Sydney!"

In 1956, he told the *Sydney Sunday Telegraph* what happened next:

> *Suddenly I began crying and I felt a powerful call from the Lord to write 'Eternity.' I had a piece of chalk in my pocket, and I bent down right there and wrote it. I've been writing it at least fifty times a day ever since, and that was thirty years ago. The funny thing is that before I wrote it I could hardly write my own name. I had no schooling, and I couldn't have spelled 'Eternity' for a hundred quid. But it came out smoothly, in a beautiful copperplate script. I couldn't understand it, and I still can't. I've tried and tried, but 'Eternity' is the only word that comes out in copperplate.*[203]

For twenty-three years, Arthur Stace had tagged his city with one perfectly written word: *Eternity*.

Everybody could see it, but the 'eternity man' remained a mystery until 1956.

On January 1, 2000, as the entire world watched television to see whether the millennium bug would affect the first major city to enter the new century, the word lit up in fireworks on Sydney Harbor Bridge, and the Australian broadcaster is reported to have spoken the following words:

> *'Eternity' is in memory of Arthur Stace who was once an alcoholic but became a born again Christian.*[204]

Do not be deceived—whatever you sow, you will reap.

And God will add a supernatural blessing so that what little you sow will echo into eternity.

ideas to consider

Picture the future harvest.

Seeing your life as a seed, picture what your actions and values will reap. Envision a future where the world is a better place—a future where the values you believe in are evident and influential. Now write those values in the cloud, and consider ways that you can sow them today.

KINGDOM PRINCIPLE 6 ❖ HUMBLING AND EXALTING

I vow to bow the knee in humility for His purposes, knowing that He will knight me, anoint me, and exalt me in His Kingdom.

shiny

Do we really need knights of the Kingdom Principles? Why would God want to raise up heroes anyway? Should we not look to God rather than man?

The simple answer is: *Knights inspire us!*

God is looking for those He can lift up as a model for what He can do in and through people's lives. We are made in the *image* of God for a reason. We help others *imagine* God. We can be examples of His character and of His dream.

Have you ever noticed that the Apostle Paul followed Jesus' example in many ways except one? Paul was a Jew, he was a teacher, he made disciples, he shared the gospel, he healed the sick, he performed miracles, yet he never told parables.

Why? Because people were his parables.

Jesus used stories, fables, and other forms of parables to demonstrate what the Kingdom of God would look like. Paul did not. Speaking several years later than Jesus, Paul was now able to use the human examples that the early Church was beginning to produce.

We sometimes forget how significant people can be to the advancement of the Kingdom, and by doing so, we put all the responsibility on God. It is too easy.

We pray for a move of God when, in reality, God is praying for a move of man.

The Kingdom of God broke through with Jesus, didn't it?

No. It broke through with John.

> From the days of John the Baptist until now, the kingdom of heaven has been forcefully advancing, and forceful men lay hold of it.[205]

The King wants knights in shining armor to come to the rescue of His people. He *is* looking for heroes. He is looking for those men and women who will live above the line and exhibit the very qualities that He is hoping to see in all of us.

The problem comes when we try to be the hero on our terms instead of His.

shotgun

Sometimes culture develops through the little things.

Over the years, I have had many comments from those outside of Pais about the culture of our organization. In particular, they highlight the servant-heartedness of our members. Authority and servanthood are important themes to Pais.

For some reason, whenever a Pais team gets into a car, whoever is senior always gets to ride 'shotgun.' It may sound silly and I'm not sure when that began, but it is part of our culture. We honor leaders because we honor the One who gave them to us. We honor authority, and by doing so, we honor the One who put it into place.

Honoring authority may be counter-cultural, but it causes us to stand out enough to make a difference. We cannot attempt to make a difference without being part of the flow of authority. We cannot allow pride in all its shapes and shades to throw us off course.

One of the first things those who join the movement discover is that even if they don't think their attitude toward authority is important, God does.

The things we think are silly and little are often big and significant to Him.

And He's the boss.

deodorant

Sometimes fact is stranger than fiction.

I know of a woman who worked in a pharmacy in the south of England. One day a well-dressed elderly lady approached the counter and asked, "Where can I purchase a bottom deodorant?"

Obviously bemused, the shop assistant gently explained that there was no such thing as a bottom deodorant. The customer, however, insisted that not only did the product exist but that she had purchased one previously from that very store and had been using it for the past few months. The pharmacist, realizing that there was no convincing the woman, punched the words 'bottom deodorant' into her computer search engine in order to prove that such an item did not exist in their inventory. No results. But the woman did not flinch. Her conviction was unshaken.

Finally, the manager was drawn into the bizarre situation and, with the aim of reassuring the customer, he walked her through every aisle. His intention was to finally, and very gently, march her out the front door once she was convinced that her quest was fruitless.

The plan did not work. Halfway down one of the aisles, the lady stopped and exclaimed, "There it is! A bottom deodorant!"

To the astonishment of the manager and the assistant, she drew their attention to an underarm deodorant, pointing to the base of the stick where you press upwards to raise the deodorant from its plastic container. Highlighting the words clearly marked on the case, she said, "Look, it says so on the label: *'Push-up bottom.'*"

The woman had misread the label.

Concerning the question of who is the greatest, we are also likely to misread the packaging. When the prophet Samuel was appointing a king, God's Spirit reminded him of an eternal truth.

> *"Do not consider his appearance or his height, for I have rejected him. The LORD does not look at the things man looks at. Man looks at the outward appearance, but the LORD looks at the heart."* [206]

To think that position gives us importance is to misread the label. And, as we will see later, that could lead to a great deal of embarrassment.

A Pais Hub Leader recently made a keen observation of human nature:

> Instead of going the *extra mile*, we go a *different mile*. Rather than putting our energy into what our leader tells us to do, we stretch ourselves in an area more comfortable to us but not helpful to them.[207]

The King, I assure you, is looking for knights. But His manner of choosing them may at times be unfamiliar to us. Culturally, we swing from one extreme to another. Either we celebrate those whose faces adorn billboards and magazines, or we instead point to those who clean our toilets or work behind the scenes, identifying them as the 'true heroes.'

But are either true? Are they not just two ends of the same line?

Is our role or position, fame or anonymity, really that important?

Is that where we should put our energy, or are we in danger of the different mile?

The problem I have in leading a missionary-making movement is that many want to be where their heroes are, but less want to walk the path that leads there. The specific quality that God is looking for is not where many of us put our energies.

He is not looking at our skills or abilities. He is not interested in our popularity and personality.

He is looking inwardly . . . for a hidden quality.

strike

The power of this hidden quality first became apparent to me as a teenager. In Britain in the late 1970s, strikes were all the rage. The miners protested the closure of coal pits and disruption spread to various other industries. There were shortages of food in shops, and some public transport ground to a halt. In fact, the trend even spread to my all-boy high school.

One day the entire campus of several hundred students decided to go on strike. The plan was that at the end of our lunchtime, when all the boys were in the schoolyard, we would all refuse to re-enter the school buildings. The proposal spread and when the bell rang signaling the end of lunchtime, everyone stayed put. Several hundred boys gathered in the schoolyard and stood in solidarity together. Perhaps a few were trying to make some kind of point by standing with their fathers and mothers against 'the man.' For most of us, however, it was just a bit of fun.

I will always remember what happened next, but before I share the story, I need to give you some context.

teachers

There were some real characters in my school, and most of them were teachers. I will not mention names in order to protect the guilty.

Mr. M's nickname was 'Mad M the Snapper.' In the first book of this series, in a section called 'snapper,' I tell the story of the time he beat me up. He was famous for having a short temper. But in some ways, it made him one of the lads.

Mr. M was cool because no one would mess with him.

Mr. C was an anarchist as well as an English teacher. He wore a black suit, black shirt, black tie, and black Doc Martins. He seemed to target the members of the Christian Union, forcing them to read out passages from a book with bad language and then punishing those who refused. His chosen method on at least one occasion was the 'kosh,' a form of corporal punishment that involved a leather strap with slits striking your hand or backside.

Mr. C was cool because he was tough.

Mr. W taught physical education. Another popular teacher, he used humor to connect with his class. Unfortunately, I still have in my mind some of the dirty jokes he told us in his classroom.

Mr. W was cool because he was witty.

Mr. N taught religion which did not particularly enhance his cool factor. Yet, Simon Newbury had a huge influence on a small group that might have been seen as his disciples. His teaching and passion had led some of the young people to trust in Jesus. He was so desperate to get us involved in the family of God that he would make multiple runs from the school gates to the local church on Friday nights, sometimes even squeezing the smaller boys into the trunk of his car.

Mr. N was not cool.

Back to the day of the strike . . .

The school authorities panicked, not sure what to do. This had never happened before. They had of course broken up small groups of boys surrounding a fight, but this was altogether more serious.

I remember Mr. M, Mr. C, and Mr. W being sent individually to address us en masse.

Speaking loudly to the entire group, each tried using his charisma to either frighten or encourage us to break our strike.

They used humor, coercion, and even threats.

All three failed.

Then Simon Newbury was sent out. I remember watching him and being puzzled because he said nothing for about a minute. Instead, he seemed to scan the crowds.

With a gut-wrenching feeling that made my stomach drop, I suddenly realized what he was doing.

He was scanning the faces for those of us in the Christian Union that he led. Just as I tried to edge behind some other students, our eyes connected. Mr. Newbury, rather than raising his voice to the whole school, took the short walk over to where I was standing and then in a lowered voice said:

"Come on, you know this is wrong."

I and, I think, one or two of my friends were the ones to break the strike that day. At great risk to our own coolness, we sheepishly stepped forward and followed Mr. Newbury past our peers towards the school door. Within two or three minutes, the entire yard had emptied.

The strike was over.

That is the power of a knight.

coke

There is one thing that Jesus never healed.

He made the blind see, the deaf hear, and the lame walk. He raised the dead from the grave and comforted those in physical and emotional pain. But this one thing He never cured:

Character.

He suddenly transformed people, commanding them to walk, to see, to hear, and to rise, but never in a moment altered them to be gentle, humble, honest, or courageous.

There are some miracles that Jesus *performs*. And others that He *processes*.

The miracle He does within our character takes time. In fact, sometimes it is time itself that fashions it.

No other teacher could have done what Simon Newbury did that day. Mr. M, Mr. C, and Mr. W were cool, but the cool teachers could not break the strike because those who followed them valued their coolness too highly. It was impossible to get them to do anything uncool.

The Kingdom of God broke into my school through Mr. N. Mr. Newbury brought hope. But where does hope come from?

> . . . *We know that suffering produces perseverance; perseverance, character; and character, hope.*[208]

Hope comes from character.

There is a difference between charisma and character.

When charisma walks into a room, everyone notices. Everyone follows. Everyone is excited. However, if it is charisma alone, they will quickly become disillusioned. Without substance, those followers will soon drop away.

When character walks into the room, nobody notices. Nobody follows, and definitely no one gets excited. But eventually that character shows through, and over a period of time, people do take notice. A leader with character will find that their followers grow gradually and will continue to follow them. Do you wonder if you possess character? Ask yourself, 'Are more people following me now than before?'

Character brings hope. People with character keep their word. They are reliable. You can trust them. When they say they will do something, you have assurance that it will happen. They turn up. They turn up on time. They arrive when they say they will arrive, and they don't leave until what they say they will do has been accomplished.

"It is finished." [209]

My problem is that so many people try to advance the Kingdom of God by putting their primary effort into developing their charisma. It's quick and it's easy.

Pour a can of Coca-Cola into a glass and something exciting happens. A lot of fizz bubbles up. It is the fizz that gets your attention. It is the fizz that overflows.

However, the fizz also dissipates.

Pour a can of Coca-Cola into a glass and something begins to build. The liquid rises up. It is the liquid that refreshes. It is the liquid that quenches thirst.

The liquid, not the fizz, is the *real thing*.

Likewise, it is the character of a knight, not the shiny armor, which impresses God.

Charisma is very useful, but on its own it will dissipate and disappoint a great deal of people. In a society that values fifteen minutes of fame, we are to go against the grain and not look for fame because our Lord is looking for something deeper than that. We are not to seek instant success because our King is looking to fashion something more long-term than that.

He's looking for the real thing.

Will you go the *extra* mile in character or the *different* mile in charisma?

naches

God needs knights who have both charisma and character, and the Kingdom Principle *Humbling and Exalting* is the process of producing one from the other.

Why did God say the following words about Jesus?

> *"This is my Son—with whom I am well pleased."*[210]

He had not really done anything yet! No miracles, no healings, no teaching, and no famous acts of kindness.

But something was hidden within Jesus at that time that the Spirit saw—something about His heart and His nature that I believe are revealed in His first miracle.

During a wedding in Cana, Jesus performs His first sign and wonder. When the wine runs out, Mary the mother of Jesus, immediately presumes too much. She had received prophecies about her Son. She had watched Him grow, and she had witnessed Him receiving gifts from very important people. We are told that she held various things in her heart, knowing that one day a future generation would call her blessed. When the wine runs out, the thought running through her mind is fairly obvious . . .

> *This is my moment!*

Here and now at a big occasion in front of all her friends and relatives would be the moment that Jesus did her proud. It was time to receive *naches*.

Naches is a Yiddish word that means 'the kind of joy only a mother feels.'

Jesus, however, reacts to this. He sees the pride within her, and using a Hebrew idiom, He politely, but firmly, challenges her motives.[211] He is also helping her to see Him as Lord, not as a child that she needs to manage. She responds perfectly. She lets it go, and then she gives the best advice ever given.

> *"Do whatever he tells you."*[212]

Watch the lesson that Jesus teaches Mary.

He does not use His gifting for party tricks or to impress His family or His disciples. In fact, only when asked does Jesus respond, and a wonderful miracle takes place. There are many things to learn here

Jesus says, *"My time has not yet come."*[213]

He was conscious of His preparation. Thirty years of preparation for three years of world-changing impact!

Jesus valued the process.

Do I?

Jesus protected the process.

Do I?

Jesus did not rush the process.

Do I?

Jesus knew the process.

Do you?

questions to ask

I am made in the image of God, so does my life help others imagine God?

If so, what do they see?

Do I want my life and words to inspire others?

Are anonymity and humility the same thing?

Could I be a parable that Jesus tells?

Do I try to be the hero on my terms instead of His, and if so . . . how?

Do I honor strangers but disrespect those closest to me?

How might I have misread the label of 'humility'?

Have I gone a *different* mile instead of the *extra* mile?

How does my character produce hope in others?

What process am I going through right now that might be a sign of God developing His character within me?

Is my life just a lot of fizz . . . or am I the real thing?

questions to add:

vigil

Knights are first squires.

Only after a squire had learned his lessons well could he hope to become a knight. Although the procedure changed over the years, a soldier was seldom knighted instantly on a battlefield. Usually, he went through a process.

The process, known as vigil, began with prayer. The squire would fast, make confession, and pray to God all night in the chapel, readying himself for life as a knight. Symbolizing purity, he was dressed in a white shirt, gold tunic, and purple cloak. After doing so, he would take the oath, vowing to obey the regulations of chivalry and to never flee from battle. Only then was he knighted by his king or lord.

A vigil is the time of preparation before the King raises you to a new position and opportunity in the Kingdom. A special process must take place to shape the heart.

Simply put, knights must first bow the knee.

Jesus explains this concept in a parable, instructing His listeners to take a humble position at a wedding feast. By taking an important place, Jesus teaches, you might be embarrassed when your host asks you to make room for more important guests at the table. But if you take a humble position, you may be blessed when he invites you to move closer to the wedding party.

Jesus concludes the story with the Kingdom Principle of *Humbling and Exalting*:[214]

> *"For everyone who exalts himself will be humbled, and he who humbles himself will be exalted."* (NIV)

> *"For whosoever exalteth himself shall be abased; and he that humbleth himself shall be exalted."* (KJV)

> *"For those who exalt themselves will be humbled, and those who humble themselves will be exalted."* (NLT)

The command is to be humble, preferring others to yourself.

The consequence is that, as you exercise humility, God will put a spotlight on you in order to demonstrate His goodness. Yet if you become proud, He will either remove you from an exalted position or stop you from getting there in the first place.

If *Reaping and Sowing* is the *futuristic* principle, then *Humbling and Exalting* is the *freedom* principle.

This principle guides us between two extremes. At one end of the line is false humility, and at the other end is pride.

When it comes to modeling God, line-dwellers are inhibited by *their* questions:

> *How do I avoid the limelight in order to avoid personal humiliation?*
> *How do I avoid anonymity in order gain personal recognition?*
> *How do I avoid the process in order to jump to the top?*

Cloud-dwellers, however, are inspired by *His* questions:

> *Will you serve an imperfect leader in order to become a perfect servant?*
> *Will you serve Me, not people, in order to bring glory to Me, not you?*
> *Will you demonstrate faithfulness so that I can show Myself faithful?*

To live above the line is to live in freedom.

Line-dwellers feel the need to impress, as though their destiny lies in the hands of others. Driven by the need to suck up to those in high positions, they ignore those who are not. They do not experience the security of knowing that no man or woman will ultimately determine whether we rise or fall.

In contrast, cloud-dwellers are free to be themselves, trusting God to shine a spotlight on them for His glory at the appropriate time.

The feudal system divided society into two classes—positions with status and positions without.

Knights had status. They occupied an important place in the jigsaw puzzle of that society, but they battled to feel valued, affirmed, and respected.

In the inside out Kingdom of God, His knights do not pursue those things.

His knights know they are valued, they feel affirmed, and they understand their importance as children of God.

Knights of the Kingdom do not fight to gain status.

They fight because they already have it.

freedom

God grants us a choice between two forms of freedom:

> freedom *from* choice
> freedom *of* choice

One is closer to the heart of God than the other.

In the Old Covenant, He shaped a community to display His glory and justice by giving them a freedom *from* choice. He set up rules and regulations, stipulations and systems.

Under the New Covenant, God compels people forward, demonstrating His glory and grace by giving us a freedom *of* choice. He lays out principles and parables, and supervision through the Spirit.

In this brave new world:

> *Everything is permissible—but not everything is beneficial. Everything is permissible—but not everything is constructive.*[215]

Suddenly, our relationship with God is emphasized, because the questions that come to our minds are:

> Beneficial to *whom?*
> Constructive to *what?*

Our freedom, it seems, comes from our status as friends of Jesus.

As Jesus walked with His disciples, He told them that He no longer called them servants, because a servant did not know his master's business. Instead, He said, *"I have called you friends."*[216]

As God moves us forward in our understanding of Him through the five covenants made with man, He also entrusts us with greater freedom. Freedom *of* choice is closer to the heart of God than freedom *from* choice.

Freedom *from* choice is comfortable, but it does not grow us as much as freedom *of* choice. It does not teach us as much about ourselves.

When we have freedom *from* choice, we have to fulfill certain commandments. Yet it is not always clear if we are fulfilling those commandments in faith and with the right motive.

Freedom *of* choice, on the other hand, teaches us much about ourselves. When we have freedom *of* choice, the decisions we make show us who we are. They show us how much we truly value our friendship with Jesus.

Did we choose the thing that most advanced the Kingdom?

Whom did it benefit and *what* did it construct?

As we are exalted, God grants us more freedom. For instance, Pais apprentices have freedom *from* choice because their team leader organizes their days and many of their objectives are already set. Pais staff members, however, have freedom *of* choice. They get to choose how to spend their time and have far more choice over the goals they set.

For the most part, I'm only able to see into the hearts of Pais workers when they become staff. Some do very well fulfilling their daily instructions, but the freedom to manage their day and the schedule of others separates the men from the boys. Once they have this freedom, what is really in their hearts comes out. Do they choose to spend their day behind a desk just managing others? Or do they choose to go out and lead, stretching themselves and others?

Do they use their freedom to make a difference or to live a comfortable life?

> *The most significant thing you will ever do is the one thing that no one ever tells you to do.*[217]

This freedom, however, comes with both a caution and a promise.

The caution:

> *"If you want to test a man, make him a failure, but if you really want to test a man, make him a success."* —Abraham Lincoln

The promises, which are many, follow in the next chapter, but before we go there, let's make sure we understand the crux of this principle and the process attached to it.

Let's start with the question: What is *true* humility?

pie

Humility is defined as 'a lack of vanity or self-importance.'[218]

But is it?

Listen to the words of Paul, a man who preached freedom.

> *I am the least of the apostles.*[219]
> *I am the very least of all the saints.*[220]
> *I am the foremost sinner.*[221]
> *Paul, called to be an apostle of Christ.*[222]
> *Therefore I urge you to imitate me.*[223]

Paul, it seems, understood that the humility Jesus seeks allows us to describe ourselves as both sinner and saint.

When someone 'eats humble pie,' we mean they have been humbled.

The phrase originated in medieval times during the age of feudalism, lords, serfs, knights, and peasants. When the aristocracy had a successful hunt, the game was prepared by the cook who would cut it into pieces and use the choice cuts of meat to prepare a feast. What was leftover from the animal—the gizzards and entrails, although not particularly tasty—were known as the 'umbles,' and were given to the servants in the form of a pie. The connection was obvious, and soon the metaphor was born.

But humility is not humiliation!

True humility is to have a right understanding of who you are before God and men.

I heard of a little girl who gave her parents a fright when they could not find her during a particularly vicious lightning storm. Frantically trying to find her in order to get the family safely to their storm shelter, they discovered her with her face pressed close to a glass window.

"Look, Daddy! God is taking a photograph of me!"

Humility knows we are special, but only through the viewfinder of an awesome God.

So what is false humility?

False humility hides behind humility.

For example, in my early twenties, I was speaking in schools, in pubs, and on the streets of my hometown of Manchester. When a friend asked me if I ever wanted to preach in church, I told him I had been asked several times but had turned the opportunity down because I was concerned that I would not be good enough.

He seemed shocked.

"Wow," he said. "You are so full of pride."

Rather indignantly, I explained that he must have misheard my reasons. He replied that he had not, and that he considered me proud because I was obviously more concerned with what people thought of my ability than how God could use it.

Ouch!

He was, of course, correct. I was using the idea of humility as spiritual camouflage to hide my true feelings.

Ever hid like that?

mechanism

The Kingdom Principle *Humbling and Exalting* is not about feeling lowly and insignificant; instead it teaches how we can bring glory to God rather than to ourselves.

A key mechanism for this principle is fairly simple: We first serve another person's vision, and then God raises others up to serve ours. At the right time, the transfer will take place.

The right time, however, does not come through experience, but through understanding. This leaves many people out. They presume that age, experience, or qualifications automatically mean promotion.

However, only when we have *understood* God better through serving will He move us forward for His purposes.

Let me give you some examples.

prince

Moses was a prince who thought the calling of God, upbringing, and position gave him the right to behave how he liked.

God humbled him.

Moses served Jethro. As he was being humbled, he learned humility, and although he was trained as a prince, he faithfully looked after sheep.

> *Now Moses was tending the flock of Jethro his father-in-law, the priest of Midian, and he led the flock to the far side of the desert and came to Horeb, the mountain of God.*[224]

Then he was exalted.

> *There the angel of the Lord appeared to him in flames of fire from within a bush.*[225]

His exaltation was a process, and understanding came through an awkward conversation with God.

Moses is an example even today of God's redemption.

tent

Joshua served Moses.

He humbled himself.

> *Then Moses would return to the camp, but his young aide Joshua son of Nun did not leave the tent.*[226]

He was then exalted.

> *So the LORD said to Moses, 'Take Joshua son of Nun, a man in whom is the spirit, and lay your hand on him.'*[227]

In the presence of God, he received wisdom, the courage to serve, and the understanding to step forward when the time was right.

Joshua is still an example of God's courage in an age of compromise.

spear

David served Saul.

> *David came to Saul and entered his service. Saul liked him very much, and David became one of his armor-bearers. Then Saul sent word to Jesse, saying, "Allow David to remain in my service, for I am pleased with him." Whenever the spirit from God came upon Saul, David would take his harp and play. Then relief would come to Saul; he would feel better, and the evil spirit would leave him.*[228]

David humbled himself.

He bent the knee even after being anointed as the future king.

During this process, Saul threw a spear at David in a fit of rage and jealousy.[229] The Bible records this because it is significant. According to ancient custom, if a master threw a spear or dart at a servant and the weapon missed, the man would be released from service.[230] Yet David willingly remained his servant. He had the right to leave, but David was a man with a heart after God's. A Kingdom Principle trumped his personal rights.

He was exalted.

> "When all the elders of Israel had come to King David at Hebron, he made a compact with them at Hebron before the LORD, and they anointed David king over Israel, as the LORD had promised through Samuel."[231]

David left us an example of God's passion, and we still sing his songs today.

feet

Jesus served the Father.

Serving the Father sounds epic, glorious, and noble. We could all serve well when the one we serve is so worthy of our service. Yet another Kingdom Principle has already taught us that we cannot serve God without serving people.[232]

> "Now that I, your Lord and Teacher, have washed your feet, you also should wash one another's feet."[233]

I can get my mind around a King who spreads out His arms and dies for the sins of the world. It is majestic. It is grandiose.

What I struggle with is this: the King of kings wore diapers.

Jesus, God incarnate, humbled Himself.

No one did it for Him.

He is exalted:

Therefore God exalted him to the highest place and gave him the name that is above every name.[234]

He submitted Himself to the same principle that also guided the disciples, Paul, and Timothy.[235]

Jesus gave us an example of God's love, and today the world sets its calendar by Him.

star

Satan served himself.

Pride resulted in the downfall of Satan, and pride resulted in the first sinful act.

> *How you have fallen from heaven,*
> *morning star, son of the dawn!*
> *You have been cast down to the earth,*
> *you who once laid low the nations!*
> *You said in your heart,*
> *"I will ascend to heaven;*
> *I will raise my throne*
> *above the stars of God . . ."*
> *But you are brought down to the grave,*
> *to the depths of the pit.*[236]

The Hebrew for *morning star* is transliterated as 'Lucifer' in the Latin vulgate. Theologians have expressed the idea that Satan was originally the worship leader of heaven.

Yet pride put an altogether different kind of spotlight on him.

The fame of serving God as the epitome of worship led to his downfall. Now infamous, the devil serves as the ultimate warning.

Pride is the eternal curse.

things to learn

Knights are first squires. Simply put, they must first bow the knee.

The King desires for me to be humble, preferring others to myself.

As I exercise humility, God will put a spotlight on me to demonstrate His goodness.

If I become proud, He will either remove me from an exalted position . . .

Or, He will stop me from getting there in the first place.

To live above the line is to live in freedom.

God grants us a choice between two forms of freedom:

> The freedom *from* choice

> The freedom *of* choice

Freedom of choice is closer to God's heart and teaches us more about ourselves.

Humility is not humiliation.

True humility is to have a right understanding of who I am before God and men.

False humility hides behind humility.

The key mechanism for this principle is that we first serve another person's vision.

Then God will raise others up to serve ours.

Pride is the eternal curse.

additional notes:

cup

Question: Can you model a life like this?

A life where you no longer put others down in order to lift yourself up. No need to compete. No need to fight. Instead, you know that God will happily raise you up in order to show you off.

A life where you do not compromise your character for love of status or finance, but you humbly and authentically submit in a less prosperous position, confident that you will be promoted in the King's eyes.

A life where you deny the desire to be needed by others and release your position to someone who can do it better than you, knowing that if you do, the Lord of all opportunities will open up a better door for you.

How much respect would that bring?

Pride comes before a fall.

But what comes before pride?

During the Last Supper, Jesus predicts Peter's denial of Him. In fact, He predicts that *all* will fall away. However, Peter's sin is singled out because of his pride. It serves as a warning to us.

Peter's pride is significant. He sees himself separated from three things.

First, he separates himself from the other disciples.

Even though he just drank from the single cup of the Passover, Peter has already forgotten the commitment he made. Drinking from this cup emphasized a communal relationship. History reveals that when the Jews drank from this one cup, they entered a covenant with each other. Their participation declared:

We will share a common destiny for good or ill.[237]

Yet Peter immediately decides his destiny will be separate from all the other disciples whom Jesus said would desert Him.

Secondly, he separates himself from the scriptures.

Jesus has just quoted from Zechariah, a book prophesying that the Messiah is to be sold for thirty pieces of silver, betrayed for the price of a potter's field, and forsaken by His disciples. Yet Peter's pride will not allow him to see himself as part of that story.

Thirdly, he separates himself from the superiority of Jesus.

Peter flatly tells Jesus He is wrong. His pride is ironic. Essentially, he is saying:

> *"I believe in You so much, that I don't believe You."*

Pride comes before a fall . . .

But separation comes before pride.

Servanthood is a natural conveyor belt. As we serve others, God brings still others to serve us in our service of Him. There is a flow of usefulness, a stream of significance, which we should never jump off or jump out of.

It leads us to a question:

What or who are you separating yourself from?

cross

Incarnation is the opposite of separation.

Jesus connected Himself to the disciples, the scriptures, and the authority of the Father.

Yet, even the humility of Jesus was not completed in an instant.

> *Although he was a son, he learned obedience from what he suffered.*[238]

History tells us something of what Jesus faced through His suffering.

We know that the Romans had three main structures for crucifixion—the 'X,' the 'T,' and the cross-shaped stakes. We know Jesus died on the cross-shaped tree because only this one had room for the sign which the Romans hung above His head.[239]

We know that He faced the torture of the forty stripes minus one. The Romans had determined a man could take only a certain number of strikes of a whip that had pieces of metal and bones embedded in it. The whip would rip a man's skin as it slid backwards off his body from wrapping around his waist.

We know that sometimes a dying body would be left to be eaten by wild animals or finally burned, but in Jesus' case, He was proven dead by a spear plunged into His side which produced water not blood.

I could go on, but I won't.

Suffice it to say that others being led to crucifixion were said to be so fearful that their pale faces appeared ghostlike. And some were so terrified that they lost the use of their legs, the ability to speak, and even their minds.

Jesus came.

Jesus wept.

Jesus learned.

Knights first bow the knee, and then they arise!

If you are determined to pursue Jesus' Kingdom Principles, then please learn the following lesson. Many want to be where Jesus is, but few want to walk the path He walked to get there.

There are many lessons within this principle, and each one comes with a promise.

benched

Lesson #1: *Humble yourself, and you will become the better you that you can be.*

Jesus had limited space and time while He walked this earth as a man. He shared only what was most important . . . and he never once talked about gifts or abilities.

So why do we?

We mistakenly think the parable of the talents is a lesson about abilities, but it is not. It is a story about character. It speaks of faithfulness.

Yet we have made skills and abilities our primary concern. We love personality tests and self-appraisals about spiritual gifts. Somehow, we have kidded ourselves into believing that the key to success lies in discovering what we should *do* rather than who we should *be*.

If life were a sporting game, character would be left sitting on the bench. We choose personality, gifts, or abilities for the key positions, believing they are the star players that will bring us victory.

When things go badly, we are forced to bring out the substitute: our character.

I wonder what would happen if instead we made character our team captain?

If we do so, the Kingdom Principle *Humbling and Exalting* promises that God can shape us into the people He created us to be.

hang

Lesson #2: *Humble yourself, and God will fill your heart with courage.*

Fear of man is as common as the common cold and just as hard to find a cure for.

True humility is the cure and is produced in the laboratory of perspective.

Sir Winston Churchill was once asked, "Doesn't it thrill you to know that every time you make a speech, the hall is packed to overflowing?"

"It's quite flattering," replied Churchill. "But whenever I feel that way, I always remember that if instead of making a political speech I was being hanged, the crowd would be twice as big."

People are fickle.

God is not.

Timidity disappears when we realize who we are before God. With His perspective, we no longer put our trust in the popularity of people, but in His character and His principles.

Courage arrives when insecurity exits.

You can exalt yourself of course, but when God does it, I promise you will feel much more secure, sleep better at night, and have the courage needed to see God's Kingdom grow *in* and *through* you.

sketchboard

Lesson #3: *Humble yourself, and you will reap the reward of every principle.*

When I was training in the 1980s, a mentor taught me a method of street preaching called 'sketchboard.' I would paint a simple picture on a board and people would gather. Although this method may seem dated now, it worked then, and it meant I did not have to shout at people passing by as some are in the habit of doing. People were intrigued. Before painting the final section, I would turn to the crowd and say, "I guess you would like to know what I am doing here."

Then I would begin my talk and offer to pray with people at the end. They would signal their intention by taking a leaflet from me.

The first time I had the opportunity to speak, I was scared to death. I prayed and fasted, prayed some more, fasted again, and memorized my notes from morning till night. I stood on the street, opened my mouth, and a few moments later several people took leaflets and prayed. I was over the moon.

My mentor suggested I speak the next day.

This time I was confident in my ability. I prayed once and did not fast. I already knew my message and did not need to go over my notes more than once.

I turned to the gathered crowd and said the words, "I guess you would like to know what I am doing here." And then . . .

My mind went *totally* blank.

I waffled. I panicked. I couldn't even remember what I was doing there!

Eventually people wandered off mid-talk. I was left preaching in the middle of the city centre to the converted. Actually, to the convert—my mentor. Even the team had disappeared!

The humble *stay* teachable.

The teachable grow in every one of the six Kingdom Principles and, therefore, they reap all of their promises.

hermit

Lesson #4: *Humble yourself, and you will become attractive.*

The story is told of a monastery where all the monks were getting old. They worried that no younger men would continue their work. As the monks tended public gardens, people on picnics would see their work and chat with them, but none would join.

Because the monastery was in danger of closing, the monks decided to visit a hermit known for hearing God. They shared their story and asked him to pray for them. The hermit prayed but did not receive an answer to their dilemma. He did mention, however, that God informed him that one of them was an apostle.

Although disappointed that God had not provided an answer, their conversation soon turned to the subject of the secret apostle. Which one of them could it be? There was much conjecture, but no decision. It was a mystery.

Concerned that they must treat the apostle well, they decided to honor every member as though he might be the one chosen. All would be treated with respect. All would be spoken of with high regard.

The picnickers saw the difference. Many of the young men began to join, sensing an exciting new community. The monastery was saved.

> *"Be devoted to one another in brotherly love. Honor one another above yourselves."* [240]

I encourage you never to serve a leader begrudgingly.

Either serve well or move on.

Better to humble yourself under a new leader you believe in than to compromise yourself for the sake of money or status.

I once heard a youth minister at a conference ask advice from a guru of youth leadership. He shared how he served in a church where the pastor was old-fashioned and narrow-minded, but everyone seemed to love him.

Without skipping a beat, the experienced man told him to resign. He warned him not to serve a man he could not believe in. The youth minister was surprised, especially as his question seemed more like an opportunity to brag rather than a genuine question.

Better to find another leader than to suffer the consequences.

God has no interest in mercenaries.

He is not impressed with those who see their own service as a stepping stone to something else, always keeping their options open for a better offer.

Jesus did not have good things to say about hired hands.[241]

For most of my life, I have been blessed to serve under great people, and I have seen the blessing of doing so. For a few years, I was not only leading Pais but also a church, so I purposely put myself under another leader to serve. I have learned that how I serve another leader will eventually affect how others serve me. Humility is an opportunity to shape the future!

Parents beware . . . how you talk about your boss, leader, or spouse around the dinner table will shape how your children see those in authority. Speak well of them, and you can shape the character of your child! Pass on this Kingdom Principle, and they will reap its promises.

Anyone can serve perfection. But can *you* serve imperfection?

Can I encourage you to never become so familiar with your leaders that you no longer honor them? The best ones will have transparent lives, but this means they are more likely to let you see their flaws.

> *A prophet has no honor in his hometown.*[242]

Why? Because the prophet has no honor?

No. It's because of familiarity.

Pride is unattractive, false humility is unsightly, but God can promise you this: true humility catches the eye!

paranymph

Lesson #5: *Humble yourself, and you will know a unique form of joy.*

When John the Baptist is approached by his disciples, they seem to be defending his honor, or at least his ministry. They seem to complain that the Jews are following the new kid in town, Jesus, rather than their own rabbi. Perhaps they are struggling with the reality that their status and even identity is tied to John's. If his ministry diminishes, they feel theirs will also.

None of this fazes John.

He is more in love with the Kingdom than with his ministry.

If the Kingdom is advancing, and he has to become less for this to happen, then so be it.

John's strength comes from his understanding.

In John's mind, he was the *paranymph*, the friend of the bridegroom, similar to the best man at a wedding, yet also akin to a matchmaker. The paranymph was responsible for introducing the bride to the bridegroom. He made the initial contact and, in Jesus' day, was charged with preparing the bride to meet her groom, even coaching her about the groom's likes and dislikes.[243]

At the wedding ceremony, the groom and the bride would finally meet. The paranymph's greatest joy would be the bridegroom's words when he turned to share his delight with him, telling him he had done a good job. Only the paranymph would experience this kind of thank-you.

It was a short role—one of introduction.

I wonder how many paranymphs fell in love with the bride as they spent time together? I wonder how many struggled handing her over to a third party?

John did not.

He loved the groom more than he loved the bride.

Do I?

Do you?

Humility allows your primary concern to become God's Kingdom.

ideas to consider

Picture the freedom.

The freedom to no longer compete for a sense of value. No need to fight. The freedom to live a life without compromising your character. The freedom from neediness. The freedom to empower others to do things better than you can.

Now fill in the cloud with the benefits of this kind of freedom.

THE HEART OF A KNIGHT

blank

So then, what exactly is in the heart of a knight of the Kingdom Principles?

The key is in the way they approach the King.

The Bible contains only one misleading passage. You will find it where the Old Testament stops and the New Testament starts.

There you will notice one blank page. This blank page represents the passage of time—more than four hundred years of history.

The blank page is deceptive because it implies nothing happened.

Nada. Zilch.

That could not be further from the truth.

The blank page represents what has been termed as 'the new sensitivity in Judaism.' In Hebrew thought, truth is unfolding and, during the intertestamental times, a revolution of philosophy had broken out in Israel through three awkward questions.[244]

Question #1: *Does the old compensatory system of ethics really work?*

In the Old Testament, black was black and white was white. God punished the wicked and rewarded the righteous. If you did something wrong, then bad things would happen to you; if you did something right, then God's favor would be poured upon you.

But there was a problem. Things didn't always work that way.

Even the prophets and the poets of the Old Testament could see this:

> Yet I would speak with you about your justice:
> Why does the way of the wicked prosper? Why do all the faithless live at ease?[245]

Yet Israel had hung on to this simplistic code of compensation. In their minds, if they *had* to resist temptation, then at least they could be certain of a reward. If they did not, they could be just as sure that one day they would somehow have to pay for it.

This was their morality.

Job fell foul to this basic line of thinking. His bizarre story starts when God points out to Satan the faithfulness of His servant Job. The devil is allowed to test Job's love for God. Job is put through hell, devastated by misfortune, disease, and grief. And just when things seemed like they couldn't get any worse . . .

His friends show up.

To them, it was obvious that he *must* have done something wrong to deserve this. He clearly had not played by the rules.

But could the rules be wrong?

Their compensatory system of ethics was the only guideline that Job's friends had, and it was failing them.

The problem was not simply in their doctrine, but in their theology.

Their religious code of morality was not wrong exactly. It was incomplete. Their study of God was missing an important fact: God had been having a conversation in heaven that they were unaware of.

Maybe He still is.

Question #2: *Is the old formula of morality really authentic?*

This new sensitivity in Judaism asked:

> *If someone is good simply to get a good man's reward, is he really good at all? If someone is righteous to get a righteous man's reward, were they really righteous in the first place?*

It was a deeper question than perhaps had been asked before. It was a question of *motive*. It was a question of *heart*.

And, it was a question that brought up the possibility that God could not be fooled by someone doing the *right thing* for the *wrong reason*.

Question #3: *What role does our concept of the Kingdom of God have in all of this?*

To some, the Kingdom of God had simply come to mean the people of God—the good people, not the bad people. In some circles, this was being rethought.

Was God's Kingdom a little more complex than that?

And if so, who cared?

itchy

In their moral judgment of Job, his friends were relying on a deficient system— the old system of compensatory ethics. But to their credit, many of the Jews, certain that truth is unfolding, kept on searching. Perhaps they thought, "The Torah is correct, but our interpretation of it is still in process."

It seems that within these four hundred years of the intertestamental period, the Spirit had begun to create an itch in preparation for the Son to come and scratch.

We all know what it's like to have an itch we can't reach. It's frustrating, and it makes us bristle and fidget.

Now let me ask you a question: When you are itchy and someone scratches you in the right spot, what does it bring?

Relief.

But what if that same person scratches you in the exact same spot when you are *not* itchy?

Pain.

The religious leaders who opposed Jesus had this problem.

They were simply not itchy.

Many of them were not asking any of the three questions. The old way of seeing morality needed no alternatives in their view. It was straightforward and could be easily packaged and presented by those in religious power. To them, the spiritual scratcher was meddling with things that should not be meddled with.

In their opinion, this battle need not be fought.

principles

I remember the first time I received a vision from God. By vision in this case, I simply mean an imaginary scene that played out in my head while I was praying.

To the left of my virtual peripheral vision, I saw a large palace door open and a young, non-descriptive boy sheepishly enter a gigantic throne room. My vision followed the boy as he walked across the large room, finally kneeling in front of a king. I realized that the boy, dressed in a simple suit of chain mail, was supposed to be me.

As I watched him bow in worship, I saw the king reach to his right and pull something out from behind his huge, ornate throne.

It was a shield.

Then came a sword.

And a helmet.

The vision evaporated, but I instinctively knew what it meant. If I would bow the knee to God, He would equip me with all I needed to fight for Him.

A knight is *equipped* for the quest, and one of the things Jesus equips us with is an *understanding* of His Kingdom Principles.

Being knighted by Jesus is not simply about fighting battles; it is about understanding His oath. This set of principles that He commands us to live by gives us insight into life itself. It provides us with a handle on what lies deep within the heart of the King of kings.

> *Yet a time is coming and has now come when the true worshipers will worship the Father in spirit and truth, for they are the kind of worshipers the Father seeks.*[246]

On the Pais Project, we teach our apprentices these six Kingdom Principles. We even have a knighting ceremony where we pass on the Kingdom Principle oath.

We teach a new kind of perspective. We promote a new way of training:

> Not *what* to think but *how* to think.

thinking

At twelve years old, I met Elaine. Her parents seemed quite posh, and they drove a little yellow Japanese car.

I had never noticed the popular Datsun roadster until then. Yet while dating her, I began spotting them everywhere. It was as if they had just been invented and were flooding the streets.

The Kingdom Principles are like that little yellow Datsun.

You rarely notice them at first because they usually appear subtly in stories throughout the Bible. They are not obvious because they are not often stated explicitly. But once someone or something points them out, you notice them all the time.

That is my hope for you—that you will notice a Kingdom Principle when you read an Old Testament story or when you listen to your colleague at work. I'm hoping that, when someone shares an issue with you, one of the principles will flash into your mind. I pray that the principles will flood your thinking and give you God's perspective in everything you do.

I hope you are empowered with spiritual armor and set on a new kind of quest.

In the last twenty years, Pais has trained young adults all over the world and sent them into schools, churches, and community projects.

Our hope is not to put a new type of curriculum into schools. Instead, our vision is to impact communities with a new kind of person.

One with a different Spirit, not simply a different religion.

The gospel message is more powerful when carried by those with authentic faith.

But what if this new generation is just as insecure, self-absorbed, and self-propagating as the rest of the world? What if all we have is a new take on the usual Christian programs? What if they are just enthusiastic idealists who believe in a cause, but fight for it in the same way that the world fights for theirs?

What if our strategy of mission, discipleship, and study is cutting edge . . . but our people are not?

Then these young public servants will be just as silent.

They will have no voice.

Or, should I say, no one will listen to their voice.

But we believe they can become a different kind of follower.

We believe they can learn a new way of thinking.

It seemed to work for Jesus anyway.

When Peter, one of Jesus' disciples, had to decide whether to accept non-Jews as Christians, he didn't draw from instructions that Jesus had given him in the past. Jesus had not said to him, "One day, Peter, you will meet this man called Cornelius the Centurion and this is what you will do . . . "

No. What helped him understand the will of God were the *principles* that Jesus had taught him, plus a slightly confusing dream. Jesus had spent three years teaching him *how* to think rather than *what* to think.

Three years.

Thinking.

Have we stopped thinking?

Have we settled instead for a spiritual self-help guide? Have we turned a book containing God's dream into nothing more than a Christian horoscope? Have we simply become Christian pagans who dip into scripture from time to time, hoping it will tell us what to avoid in order to live a better life?

Have we misinterpreted *favor* for a *formula?* A formula that tries to force God into giving us everything we want.

Has this led us to live a *Christianized* life? A life lived on the line. A life lived in the shadow.

What if instead we approached the King, feeling itchy, asking the question:

> *What is in Your heart?*

If our motive for entering His presence and our purpose for reading His Word are different from the pagans, then we will desire something deeper than *life* principles. We will search for *Kingdom* principles.

And in doing so, our hearts and minds will be transformed.

We will love the Kingdom more than life itself.

We will become knights who fight for the heart of our King.

Remember, God does not have favorites.

He does, however, favor those who direct their hearts toward Him.

EPILOGUE

ceremony

Jesus knighted His Church and the Church has always knighted its warriors—those who decide to live above the line, those who are set apart. We even have a name for it; we call it the 'laying on of hands':

> *For this reason, I remind you to fan into flame the gift of God, which is in you through the laying on of my hands.*[247]

On the Pais Project, we teach the Kingdom Principles at the very beginning of the year and then we create a defining moment for them—a knighting ceremony.

A room is darkened and lit only with candles. Scripture is read out by those who were previously knighted. Those wishing to participate cross a line on the floor. They bow the knee, and we lay hands on them. They are given a simple symbol to carry around their neck or wrist.

As we knight them, we give them one more thing . . .

A scroll.

It contains an oath—a vow we encourage them to take as a reminder for them after their ceremony. Some hang it on their bedroom wall, some carry it in their wallet, some keep it in their car, and others even scan it and use it as a screensaver.

We call it *The Creed and the Vow*.

vow

If this book has moved you, I challenge you to make this vow your own.

Thanks for reading. I pray for you as you seek to live life above the line and fight for the heart of your King!

God bless you.

Paul

This is my vow, to live above the line.

> But seek ye first the Kingdom of God, and His righteousness;
> and all these things shall be added unto you.

I vow to make the Kingdom of God my primary concern, knowing He will make it His to give me all I need.

> Do not judge or in the same way you judge others, you also will be judged,
> and with the measure you use, it will be measured to you.

I vow to show mercy and grace to the King's children knowing the King Himself will show grace and mercy to me.

> A good man out of the good treasure of the heart bringeth forth good things:
> and an evil man out of the evil treasure bringeth forth evil things.

I vow to be wise in the things that my eyes see, ears hear, and heart joins, knowing that the Dragon will then be slain.

> For everyone who has will be given more, and he will have an abundance.
> Whoever does not have, even what he has will be taken from him.

I vow to be faithful in the little that God has entrusted to me in order to take hold of the more that He has for me.

> Do not be deceived; God is not mocked. For whatsoever a man soweth,
> that shall he also reap.

I vow to sow seeds into my life that will produce fruit for the Kingdom of God.

> For everyone who humbles himself will be exalted,
> and he who exalts himself will be humbled.

I vow to bow the knee in humility for His purposes, knowing that He will knight me, anoint me, and exalt me in His Kingdom.

This is my vow:

> To fight for the heart of my King and to live for His Kingdom and
> according to its principles.
> So help me God.

END NOTES

Prologue

1   1 Samuel 13:14.

2   Matthew 1:1; Matthew 22:42.

3   Colossians 3:25.

4   Ephesians 6:9.

5   2 Timothy 3:16.

6   John 21:25.

The Heart of the King

7   Ephesians 6:11-12.

8   Derived from Encarta, s.v. "chivalry," published 2009, last accessed April 25, 2011. http://encarta.msn.com/encnet/features/dictionary/DictionaryResults. aspx?lextype=3&search=chivalry.

9   The film *Kingdom of Heaven*, directed by Ridley Scott (Los Angeles, California: 20th Century Fox, 2005), DVD.

10 Regarding issues of doctrine, there is a similar idea of defending a position according to a line in *A New Kind of Christian* by Brian McLaren.

11 If you don't believe me, then put 'hypnotize a chicken' into the YouTube search engine. If you try doing it yourself, be sure to video it and post it on *The Cloud and the Line* Facebook page.

12 Shekhinah is the English spelling of a grammatically feminine Hebrew language word that means the dwelling or settling, and is used to denote the dwelling or settling presence of God.

13 The cloud references are found in Exodus 13:21; Exodus 14:24; Exodus 16:10; Exodus 19:9; Numbers 9:15; Matthew 17:5; Matthew 24:30; Revelation 14:14.

Seek First | The Problem

14 Matthew 6:31-32.

15 The single 'Road to Nowhere' (from the album *Little Creatures*) was released by the American rock band Talking Heads in 1985. It reached number 25 on the Billboard Mainstream Rock Tracks and number 6 in the British and German singles chart.

16 One of my favorite speakers is the historian Ray Vanderlaan. He speaks about this road and the following details on one of his DVDs. Ray Vanderlaan, *Faith Lessons – In the Dust of the Rabbi*, Volume 6 (Grand Rapids, MI: Zondervan, 2005), DVD.

17 Ibid.

18   Ibid. Archeologists have discovered the remains of old games scratched into the pavement used to pass the time while waiting for their oracle.

19   Ibid. In other similar temples, pictures have been discovered of an oracle suspended over a similar pit where fumes would engulf her. These vapors were a strange mix of ingredients and perhaps the nearest description we would understand would lead us to believe she was essentially sniffing glue.

20   You can learn more about The Pais Project at www.paisproject.com or by reading the first book of the Kingdom Trilogy, *The Line and the Dot.*

21   Ecclesiastes 3:11.

22   Matthew 23:15 (New Living Translation).

Seek First | The Principle

23   2 Samuel 23:13-17.

24   Reinhardt Bonnke, *Plundering Hell to Populate Heaven* (Oklahoma, Harrison House Inc, 1987).

25   Matthew 6:33 (NIV 1984, KJV, NLT 1996).

26   Strong's Numbers, s.v. "3309. Basileía", accessed April 25, 2011, http://strongsnumbers.com/greek/932.htm.

27   Luke 11:1.

28   Luke 11 simply says *"Your kingdom come,"*; Matthew 6 includes *"Your will be done, on earth as it is in heaven."*

29   Luke 12:34.

30   A tithe is a one-tenth part of something, paid as a voluntary contribution usually to support a religious organization. Wikipedia, s.v. "tithe", accessed May 21, 2011, http://en.wikipedia.org/wiki/Tithe.

31   Luke 21:4.

32   1 Chronicles 21:24b.

33   Gates, Melinda French. "What nonprofits can learn from Coca Cola." Filmed September 2010 at a TEDx conference. TEDx video, 16:29. Posted October 2010. http://www.ted.com/talks/melinda_french_gates_what_nonprofits_can_learn_from_coca_cola.html.

34   Paraphrase of Proverbs 29:18.

35   Matthew 6:34.

36   Strong's Numbers, s.v. "3309. Merimnaó", accessed April 21, 2011, http://strongsnumbers.com/greek/3309.htm.

37   Stephen R. Covey, A. Roger Merrill, and Rebecca R. Merrill, *First Things First* (London, Simon & Schuster UK Ltd, 1999), 88-89.

38   Matthew 13:21-23, Mark 4:18-20, Luke 8:13-15.

39   Charles R. Swindoll, *Growing Strong in the Seasons of Life*, (Michigan, Zondervan, 1983, 2007), 293.

40   John 20:29.

Seek First | The Promise

41   In a future book I will share a letter I received from a campaign advisor for a British Prime Minister. In it he shares his belief in the power of what we do over that of politicians.

42   Ecclesiastes 4:9-12.

43   This quote from one of the major national tabloids in England was used to describe this particular neighborhood in Moston, Manchester.

44   Daniel 1.

45   Daniel 1:4.

46   Daniel 1:12-13.

47   This is the conclusion I came to after some study and an online discussion I had with Rabbi Reuven Lauffer.

Judge and Be Judged | The Problem

48   Talmud, in Judaism, is the vast compilation of the Oral Law with rabbinical elucidations, elaborations, and commentaries, in contradistinction to the Scriptures or Written Laws. The Talmud is the accepted authority for Orthodox Jews everywhere. Definition found at reference.com, s.v. "Talmud," accessed May 23, 2011, http://www.reference.com/browse/talmud.

49   Revelation 12:11. Interestingly the word translated as "... and their" is *autos* (g846 Strongs), which has connections to the word "baffle." I think we have become confused as to the meaning of this verse.

50   See video of the young man's testimony at http://www.vimeo.com/23272938.

51   Aiden Wilson Tozer, *The Knowledge of the Holy: The Attributes of God: Their Meaning in the Christian Life* (New York, Harper Collins, 1961).

52   Matthew 23:1-3.

53   Flavius Josephus; translated by William Whiston; commentary by Paul L. Maier, *The New Complete Works of Josephus* (Grand Rapids, Michigan, Kregel Publications,1999), 739.

54   This was added at the Council at Yavneh. See Dr. Ron Moseley, *Yeshua: A Guide to the Real Jesus and the Original Church* (Maryland: Messianic Jewish Resources International, 1998), 121.

55   John 13:34-35.

Judge and Be Judged | The Principle

56   Matthew 7:1-2 (NIV 1984, KJV, NLT 1996, Literal Greek).

57   Genesis 4:9.

58   Exodus 21:24 (New Living Translation, 1996).

59   Noah, see Genesis 9:9; Abraham, see Genesis 17; Moses, see Exodus 19-24; David, see 2 Samuel 7; Jesus, see Hebrews 8:6.

60   Genesis 6:9. According to Jewish teaching, Noah's righteousness was seen partly or perhaps solely in comparison to the generation in which he lived. Jewish Study Bible. Publisher: Oxford University Press, USA (January 4, 2004).

61   John 15:15.

62   Matthew 18:23-34.

63   Matthew 18:32-33.

64   2 Samuel 12:1-13.

65   In Ephesians 6, the writer unpacks various symbolic weapons of spiritual warfare. It is commonly understood that in the Roman soldier's armor there is nothing to protect his back. Frank had taken a very loose and fragile concept to beat up his brother in Christ.

66   Ephesians 5:18-19 (New Living Translation, 1996).

67   Colossians 1:24.

68   James 1:27.

69   Matthew 25:37-40.

70   Matthew 6:14-15 (New International Version, 2011).

71   1 John 4:20.

Judge and Be Judged | The Promise

72   1 Corinthians 15:33, actually quoting the Ancient Greek poet and dramatist Menander (342 BC – 292 BC).

73   *"The woman you put here with me – She gave me some fruit from the tree, and I ate it."* Genesis 3:12.

74   Proverbs 22:11.

75   African Proverb.

76   Psalm 135:14.

77   Proverbs 25:21-22.

78   Ephesians 6:11.

79   Ephesians 6:12.

80   John 13:34-35.

81   Galatians 3:28.

82   John 20:23.

83   Dr. Ron Moseley, *Yeshua: A Guide to the Real Jesus and the Original Church* (Maryland: Messianic Jewish Resources International, 1998), 25-26. This form of disqualification from service as a punishment happened many times in history and especially during the rule of Herod the Great.

84   I was inspired to create this object lesson from the example that Phillip Yancey teaches in his book *What's so Amazing about Grace* (Grand Rapids, Michigan, Zondervan, 1997), 273.

Rubbish In, Rubbish Out | The Problem

85   Revelation 12:9.

86   To see what I mean, check out www.youtube.com/watch?v=Xcv5bxUtnpE for a rather embarrassing example.

87   2 Timothy 3:2-5 (abbreviated).

88   Romans 7:15-20.

89   DL Moody quoted in TJ Shanks, *D.L.Moody at Home: His Home and Home Work* (Chicago & New York, Fleming H. Revell, 1886), 272.

90   1 Corinthians 10:13.

91   Hebrews 4:15.

92   John Maxwell, *Developing the Leader Within You: Workbook* (Nashville, Tennessee, Thomas Nelson, 1993), 42.

93   Matthew 12:43-45.

Rubbish In, Rubbish Out | The Principle

94   A.J. Jacobs, *The Year of Living Biblically: One Man's Humble Quest to Follow the Bible as Literally as Possible* (New York, Simon & Schuster, 2007), 257.

95   Matthew 12:35.

96   My friend is Derek Smith the pioneering leader of www.kingsbolton.co.uk.

97   John Wesley (1703-1791).

98   Galatians 5:19-21.

99   Galatians 5:22-24.

100 1 Corinthians 5:9.

101 1 Corinthians 6:18.

102 1 Corinthians 3:1-2.

103   1 Corinthians 3:3-4.

104   2 Corinthians 11:13.

105   Thomas Paine, *The Life and Writings of Thomas Pain*, ed. Daniel Edwin Wheeler (New York, Vincent Parke and Company, 1908), 110.

Rubbish In, Rubbish Out | The Promise

106   Rev. 12:11.

107   John 19:11; Matthew 23:23.

108   Luke 18:11.

109   ed. Geoffrey Wigoder, Fred Skolnik and Shmiel Himelstein, *The New Encyclopedia of Judaism* (New York, New York University Press, 2002).

110   R. David Kinhi in ibid.

111   You can read about Jonah's rebellion in the Old Testament book of Jonah.

112   Jonah 1:6.

113   2 Samuel 11.

114   2 Samuel 11: 1-2, 4-5.

115   Philippians 4:8.

116   Matthew 12:34.

117   Hebrews 5:12 (New King James).

118   Mark 9:47.

119   David H. Stern, *Jewish New Testament Commentary* (Clarkville, Maryland, Jewish New Testament Publications, Inc.), 16.

120   A literal translation of Lamentations 5:21 from *The Jewish New Testament Commentary*, 1989.

Use It or Lose It | The Problem

121   Matthew 25:26-28.

122   John 8:44.

123   Genesis 3:13.

124   Revelation 20:10.

125   Strongs, s.v. 635 apoplanaó, accessed May 5, 2011, http://strongsnumbers.com/greek/635.htm.

126   Matthew 25:24-25.

127   1 Peter 5:8.

128   Callipers is the English word for leg braces worn by disabled children.

129 1 Corinthians 1:27.

130 Matthew 25:15.

131 Midrash Rabbah: Genesis 39:11.

132 Ibid.

Use It or Lose It | The Principle

133 This group was the Sadducees.

134 Matthew 4:23.

135 Acts 15:28-29.

136 1 Corinthians 13:12 (Today's New International Version, 2005).

137 Matthew 25:29.

138 Luke 5:1-3.

139 1 Kings 18:25-29.

140 1 Kings 18:40.

141 1 Kings 17:2-7; 1 Kings 18:7-10.

142 1 Kings 19:8.

143 1 Kings 19:9-21.

144 1 Kings 17:1-7.

145 1 Kings 17:14-16.

146 1 Kings 17:17-24.

147 1 Kings 18:41-45; James 5:17-18.

148 1 Kings 18:24; 1 Kings 18:36-38.

149 2 Kings 1:10-12; Luke 9:54.

150 1 Kings 17:1-7.

151 1 Kings 21:17-29; 2 Kings 9:25-37.

152 2 Kings 1:2-17.

153 2 Chronicles 21:12-15.

154 Matthew 17:3-4; Mark 9:4; Luke 9:30.

155 2 Kings 9:1-3.

156 2 Kings 2:14.

157 2 Kings 4:1-7.

158 2 Kings 4:18-37.

159 2 Kings 4:38-41.

160 2 Kings 4:42-44.

161 2 Kings 5:1-19; Luke 4:27

162 2 Kings 6:6.

163 2 Kings 6:17.

164 2 Kings 4:16.

165 2 Kings 7:2.

166 2 Kings 8:1-3.

167 2 Kings 8:7-10.

168 2 Kings 8:11-15.

169 2 Kings 13:14-19.

170 2 Kings 2:1-15.

171 2 Kings 4:31.

172 2 Kings 5:25-27.

173 2 Kings 5.

174 2 Kings 6:15-17.

175 Strong's Numbers, s.v. 1522. Gehazi, accessed May 5, 2011, http://strongsnumbers.com/hebrew/1522.htm.

Use It or Lose It | The Promise

176 Rick Warren, *The Purpose Driven Life* (Grand Rapids, Michigan, Zondervan, 2002), 233.

177 Romans 8:28.

178 Acts 20: 10-12.

179 Elijah and Elisha both raised people from the dead in this manner: 1 Kings 17:17-24 & 2 Kings 4:17-37.

180 Jews and Christians originally rested on the Friday/Saturday Jewish Sabbath. Pagan Romans and Greeks did not keep a weekly rest day (in fact, they sometimes mocked Jews for this practice). However, Roman law protected the Jewish right to observe the Sabbath. There was not yet a Sunday rest custom, and Roman law would not have granted it. This probably explains Eutychus' sleepiness—he worked all day, and then joined the Jews.

181 Hebrews 11:6.

Reaping and Sowing | The Problem

182 Psalm 127:3-5.

183 Matthew 24:36, 42-44.

184 Rabbi Shmuel bar Nachmani said this in the name of Rabbi Yonaton (Sanhedrin 97b).

185 Rabbi Zera (Sanhedrin 97a).

186 This was a Arizona Bark Scorpion. For more information on them, see Wikipedia, s.v. "Arizona Bark Scorpion," accessed May 7, 2011, http://en.wikipedia.org/wiki/Arizona_bark_scorpion.

187 Matthew 25:1-13.

188 Matthew 24:45-51.

Reaping and Sowing | The Principle

189 Matthew 12:34-35.

190 Job 4:8, Proverbs 22:8, Matthew 7:17-20, Matthew 15:18, Luke 6:45.

191 Galatians 6:7.

192 Winston Churchill (1874-1965). "Churchill voted greatest Briton," BBC News, World Edition, November 24, 2002, http://news.bbc.co.uk/2/hi/entertainment/2509465.stm.

193 Luke 6:31.

194 Author Unknown.

Reaping and Sowing | The Promise

195 Numbers 14.

196 Matthew 7:17-18.

197 Luke 6:38.

198 Dr. Merrill Douglass, *Homemade*, April 1990.

199 Joel 2:25 (King James Version).

200 Psalm 126:5-6.

201 Bible.org, accessed May 7, 2011, http://bible.org/illustration/diary-john-wesley.

202 Galatians 6:9.

203 Tom Farrell, *Sydney Sunday Telegraph*, 21 June 1956.

204 Reference unknown.

Humbling and Exalting | The Problem

205 Matthew 11:12.

206 1 Samuel 16:7.

207 Chris Cunnington and his wife Emma have been on Pais for seven years. He

serves as a Hub Leader in Texas USA.

208 Romans 5:3-4.

209 John 19:30.

210 Matthew 3:17.

211 For a fuller picture of the conversation, see David H. Stern, *New Testament Commentary* (Clarkville, Maryland, Jewish New Testament Publications Inc.), 163.

212 John 2:5.

213 John 2:4.

Humbling and Exalting | The Principle

214 All three are translations of the same verse: Luke 14:11.

215 1 Corinthians 10:23 (New International Version – UK, 1973).

216 John 15:15.

217 This is a conviction of mine that I wrote in *The Line and the Dot*, 89.

218 Yahoo Thesaurus, s.v. "humility", accessed May 10, 2011, http://education.yahoo.com/reference/thesaurus/entry/humility.

219 1 Corinthians 15:9.

220 Ephesians 3:8 (English Standard Version, 2011).

221 1 Timothy 1:15 (GOD'S WORD® Translation, 1995).

222 1 Corinthians 1:1.

223 1 Corinthians 4:16.

224 Exodus 3:1.

225 Exodus 3:2.

226 Exodus 33:11.

227 Numbers 27:18.

228 1 Samuel 16:21-23.

229 1 Samuel 18:11.

230 James M. Freeman, *Manners and Customs of the Bible* (New York, Logos International, 1972), 215.

231 1 Chronicles 11:3.

232 This refers to the Kingdom Principle *Judge and Be Judged*.

233 John 13:14.

234 Philippians 2:9.

235 Matthew 23:11, 1 Corinthians 6:2-3, Acts 11:19-30, Acts 16:3, 1 Timothy 1:18.

236 Isaiah 14:12-15.

Humbling and Exalting | The Promise

237 For more on the significance of the cup, see *The NIV Archeological Study Bible,* 1655.

238 Hebrews 5:8.

239 Matthew 27:37.

240 Romans 12:10.

241 John 10:11-13.

242 Paraphrase of Matthew 13:57.

243 James M. Freeman, *Manners and Customs of the Bible* (New York, Logos International, 1972), 423.

The Heart of a Knight

244 For a deeper understanding of this phrase, read: Professor David Flusser, *The Sage From Galilee* (Grand Rapids, Michigan, WM.D.Eerdmans Publishing Company, 2007). Flusser was the Professor of Early Christianity and Second Temple Judaism at the Hebrew University of Jerusalem.

245 Jeremiah 12:1.

246 John 4:23.

Epilogue

247 2 Timothy 1:6.

about the kingdom trilogy

the line and the dot

the first in the trilogy, this book studies kingdom pioneering.

using the motif of a pioneer, it presents an alternative view of *vision* in the kingdom of God.

the cloud and the line

the second in the trilogy, this book examines kingdom principles.

using the motif of a knight, it presents an alternative view of *religion* in the kingdom of God.

the seed and the cloud

the third in the trilogy, this book analyzes kingdom patterns.

using the motif of a pilgrim, it presents an alternative view of *direction* in the kingdom of God.

www.facebook.com/thelineandthedot
www.facebook.com/thecloudandtheline
www.facebook.com/theseedandthecloud

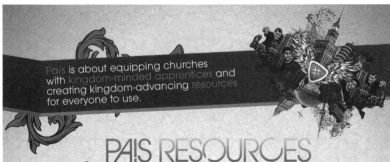

Pais is about equipping churches with kingdom-minded apprentices and creating kingdom-advancing resources for everyone to use.

PAIS RESOURCES

Now available is a selection of **books**, **mp3s** and **videos**, as well as other digital teaching series.

100% of the profits go to the work of the Pais Project

Buy online now at **www.paisproject.bigcartel.com**

DONATING TO PAIS

If you would like to **sow** into the work of the **Pais Project**, then please consider making a donation.

Every gift is **tax-deductible** and we will send you receipts for your tax return. Donations can be made **online** or via personal check.

If you would like more information about making a donation, please contact us at: globalpais@paisproject.com

PAISPROJECT
www.paisproject.com

about the author

paul gibbs is the founding & global director of pais. he is married to lynn and has two sons, joel and levi. originally from manchester, england, paul moved to the usa in 2005.

paul began pioneering openings into manchester schools as an associate minister in 1987. in september 1992 he founded the pais project. initially a vision for a one-team gap year project in north manchester, the project has exploded globally, training and placing thousands of missionaries and reaching millions of students throughout europe, north and south america, asia, and africa.

Paul has developed a new wing of Pais that equips churches in missional strategies. While continuing to direct the organization, paul has served in various other roles: director with youth alive [uk]; senior minister at thefaithworks [uk] where he launched a mentoring academy; and as a senior leader at pantego bible church [tx, usa].

paul founded global:pais, the international resource team for pais throughout the world. this team continues to grow and has since launched initiatives such as www.mypais.info, livewire online training, and other resources.

paul gained national recognition in the uk for mentoring and training leaders. he has written courses for and spoken at various bible colleges and seminaries in the uk and the states.

teaching throughout the world, his primary topics include pioneering, leadership development, the kingdom of God, and ancient practices for post-modern times.

paul enjoys swimming, surfing, skiing, sailing, snowboarding, and is an avid manchester united fan!

find out more at
www.paulgibbs.info
www.facebook.com/paulcgibbs
www.twitter.com/paulcgibbs

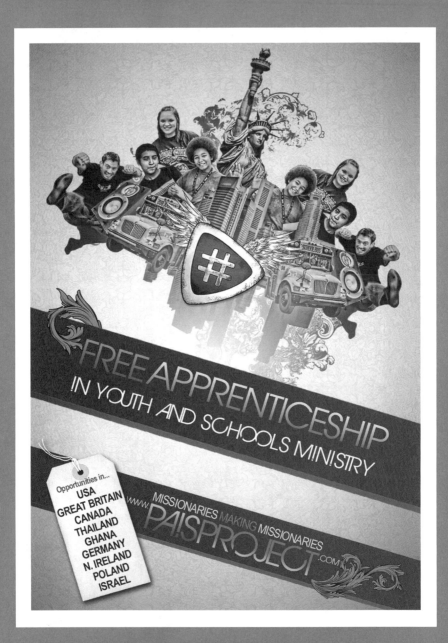

about the pais project

our aim

to spark a global movement in schools by empowering churches with kingdom-minded apprentices who serve in youth ministry and work in local schools,
building relational bridges between the two.

our motto

missionaries making missionaries

our passion

we are passionate about the young people of our world and are desperate to see
them in the relationship with God that He intended us to have. always apprecia-
tive of the school's policies and sensitive to their needs, we assist them as they
seek to help young people find their purpose. we come alongside the vision
of the local church and endeavour to empower the youth as they grow in their
understanding and experience of God.

our name

pais is the new testament greek word for child or child servant to the king.

our vision is to take the young people we disciple and help them become all they
can be.

mission lies at the heart of pais. we don't see it as a one-time event, but seek to
help both the apprentice and those they touch to develop a missionary heart,
missionary skills, and a missionary life. as each missionary makes a missionary, we
see our world change.

our details:
www.paisproject.com
www.facebook.com/paisproject
www.twitter.com/paisproject